T0219847

Understanding Microsoft Intune

Deploying Applications Using PowerShell

Owen Heaume

Apress®

Understanding Microsoft Intune: Deploying Applications Using PowerShell

Owen Heaume
West Sussex, UK

ISBN-13 (pbk): 978-1-4842-8849-8   ISBN-13 (electronic): 978-1-4842-8850-4
https://doi.org/10.1007/978-1-4842-8850-4

Managing Director, Apress Media LLC: Welmoed Spahr
Acquisitions Editor: Smriti Srivastava
Development Editor: Laura Berendson
Coordinating Editor: Mark Powers

Cover designed by eStudioCalamar

Cover image by Providence Doucet on Unsplash (www.unsplash.com)

Distributed to the book trade worldwide by Apress Media, LLC, 1 New York Plaza, New York, NY 10004, U.S.A. Phone 1-800-SPRINGER, fax (201) 348-4505, e-mail orders-ny@springer-sbm.com, or visit www.springeronline.com. Apress Media, LLC is a California LLC and the sole member (owner) is Springer Science + Business Media Finance Inc (SSBM Finance Inc). SSBM Finance Inc is a **Delaware** corporation.

For information on translations, please e-mail booktranslations@springernature.com; for reprint, paperback, or audio rights, please e-mail bookpermissions@springernature.com.

Apress titles may be purchased in bulk for academic, corporate, or promotional use. eBook versions and licenses are also available for most titles. For more information, reference our Print and eBook Bulk Sales web page at http://www.apress.com/bulk-sales.

Any source code or other supplementary material referenced by the author in this book is available to readers on GitHub (https://github.com/Apress). For more detailed information, please visit http://www.apress.com/source-code.

Printed on acid-free paper

For my family: Kate, Ella, Lana, Red, Rue, and Rhy – I love you all.

Table of Contents

About the Author xi

About the Technical Reviewer xiii

Acknowledgments xv

Who This Book Is For xvii

Introduction xix

Chapter 1: PowerShell Fundamentals...1

  Writing Code 1

  PowerShell Cmdlets...4

    It's Okay to Ask for Help 6

    Parameters 8

    Pipeline..8

    The Ten Cmdlets 9

    Scripting 16

  Summary..20

Chapter 2: MSIEXEC...21

  Fundamentals 21

    View the Help 21

    Where Is It? 23

    Better to Use $Env:...24

    Parameters 27

Properties 29

Uninstall GUIDs 33

Summary...37

Chapter 3: Setup.exe 39

Discovering the Setup.exe Silent Install/Uninstall Parameters 39

EXEs Have Registry Information Too...39

In-Built Help 40

Internet Search..41

MSI Extraction 41

Summary...46

Chapter 4: Detection Rules 47

Why Use PowerShell? 47

Detection Fundamentals 48

The Microsoft Rules..48

In Practice...49

Where Do I Put the Detection Rules Anyway? 50

Silently Continue..51

How Detection Scripts Work 53

Detection Rule Types 54

Custom Detection 65

Branching 71

This *and* This 75

Summary...76

Chapter 5: Location, Location, Location.....................................79

Where Is This Script Running from Anyway? 79

    How We Used to Do Things...80

    A Better Way 81

File Placement 81

    Flat-File Placement 81

    Structured File Placement 82

Referencing Files 84

    First Things First..84

    Referencing Files in a Flat Structure 84

    Referencing Files in Subdirectories...85

    To Me, To You, and Back Again..86

    Push/Pop-Location 89

    Let's Try This Again..90

Summary..92

Chapter 6: Installing the Application 93

Start Your Engines Please 93

Parameters..94

    -FilePath 94

    -ArgumentList...95

    -NoNewWindow..96

    -Wait 96

Dealing with Spaces 96

Putting It All Together..97

    Example 1 – Simple MSI...97

Example 2 – MSI with Properties 97

Example 3 – Setup.Exe 98

Summary..98

Chapter 7: Deploying the Script...99

Sys What Now? 99

Solution 100

32-Bit PowerShell..100

64-Bit PowerShell..101

Calling Your Script...101

Standard Script (Top to Bottom) 102

Script with Entry Point...103

Function...105

Example: Deploying a Script Containing Two Functions 108

Remote Server Administration Tools.....................................109

Summary..115

Chapter 8: Deployment Template...117

What It Does...117

The Template...118

The Template – Explained...122

Summary..128

Chapter 9: Application Preparation 129

Intunewin 129

Download the Content Prep Tool...129

Prepare to Prep...131

Adding the Content..133

Converting the Source Files..134

What's in a Name? 136

Summary 137

Chapter 10: Uninstall an Application 139

PowerShell to the Rescue 139

In Practice 141

Detecting the Old Application 142

Adding to the Template 143

Summary 143

Chapter 11: Pre- and Post-Code 145

Detect Office "Bitness" 145

Detect Operating System Architecture 147

Obtaining the Current Logged-in Username 147

Copying Files 148

Unstructured Method 148

Structured Method 150

Register/Unregister DLL Files 151

Register a DLL 152

Unregister a DLL 153

Summary 153

Chapter 12: Example Scenario 155

Notepad++ 155

Obtain the Installer 155

MSI Extraction 156

Determine the Install and Uninstall Commands 158

The Application Detection Rule 161

The Uninstall Code 164

Source File Placement..165

The File Copy Code 165

The Deployment Template 166

Dry Run...168

Create the Intunewin File 169

Application Deployment...170

Log File 177

Summary...178

Index..179

About the Author

Owen Heaume is a senior network administrator for a global company based in the UK's headquarters. He has over 20 years of networking experience across Novell and Microsoft technologies and has acquired a variety of professional technical qualifications. He enjoys writing blogs and information on ConfigMgr and PowerShell scripting. Owen has also published two books on ConfigMgr: one for deploying applications using PowerShell and one for deploying language and regional settings.

About the Technical Reviewer

Joymalya Basu Roy is an Indian IT professional with around 6.5 years of work experience in IT Software Support and Services. Having completed his B.Tech. in Computer Science and Engineering back in 2015, he is 30 years old as of 2022, ethnolinguistically a Bengali, and hails from the Indian city of Kolkata, West Bengal. Presently associated with Atos as a Senior Consultant – Architect, he works in Digital Workplace T&T projects leading the build and deployment, adoption, and support of Microsoft Intune across greenfield/brownfield environments for Android/iOS/Windows. He is also honored to be recognized as a Microsoft MVP for Enterprise Mobility – 2021 and 2022-23. You can find him blogging on the different topics of MEM through his blog site www.joymalya.com, and if you want to connect, you can find him on LinkedIn (www.linkedin.com/in/joymalyabasuroy/) and Twitter (@jbasuroy369).

Acknowledgments

It is hard to write a book when we all have such busy lives these days. I had encouragement from many people but there are a couple who deserve a special mention. I should really thank my manager, Biniam Bekit. He has always been supportive of my endeavors and is perhaps the nicest and kindest man I have ever met. Thanks, Biniam.

I must also thank my wife Kate, who put up with my short temper, stressed-out book discussions, and my 5 a.m. alarms so I could write before work. I could not have done it without your support and patience, and I love you to pieces.

Who This Book Is For

This book is for the tired and weary administrator who hasn't got the time to figure out how to deploy the next quirky application using Microsoft Intune. You may realize that this can be achieved using PowerShell but are not sure how, or perhaps you keep writing new PowerShell code for every different application deployment that comes your way.

That said, you do not require any prior PowerShell or scripting knowledge to be able to use the techniques shown in this book as everything will be explained as you read on, although some basic knowledge will enable you to skip past some teaching moments.

After reading this book, not only will you be able to deploy pretty much any application that gets thrown your way, but you will end up with an easily understood PowerShell template that is reliable and repeatable. (And gets you kudos with the boss!)

Introduction

This book came about as a requirement of my job; I am often tasked with deploying applications that are beyond a simple MSI. I was looking for a straightforward way to create reliable and repeatable deployments that can manage some of the odd scenarios I always seem to end up with.

Examples of nonstandard deployments I have been given in the past include deploying an application based on the installed bitness of Microsoft Office (32-bit or 64-bit), ensuring that certain DLL files were registered pre- or post-application deployment or that an add-in is installed and then activated in Excel.

My troubles were resolved by writing a remarkably simple PowerShell template that can be reused and very easily changed to meet the needs of almost any deployment scenario. Having said that, the knowledge contained within this book is not exclusive to having to use the supplied deployment template; it can be used in any PowerShell script you write yourself for deploying applications.

This book begins with some PowerShell fundamentals, explaining the cmdlets that are often used as customization options within the template, and some examples to get you used to them.

You will cover some crucial MSI and setup techniques which are the final steps in laying the foundation for the meat and potatoes that go into the making of the final deployment template.

You will then cover the several types of detection rules, again, using PowerShell, before moving on to where to place files for deployment.

Once that is covered you will learn about calling PowerShell scripts from Intune and why you would use one method over another.

You will learn about uninstalling programs and then move on to the deployment template itself.

Finally, there is an example that takes the entire process from start to finish.

Many of the techniques shown in this book can also be used stand-alone and you will be able to pick bits and pieces from various chapters to help you with your specific deployment goals regardless of using the template or not.

You can also use this book as a reference, which I do often, particularly Chapter 2 and Chapter 7 – you just can't remember everything and it's pretty handy. Source code used in this book can be downloaded from github.com/apress/understanding-ms-intune.

I believe I'm right when I quote from *Spider-Man*, *"With great PowerShell comes great responsibility."* Well, it's something like that anyway, so let's make a start with some PowerShell fundamentals.

CHAPTER 1

PowerShell Fundamentals

Although this book is not about to teach you how to become the next PowerShell guru (there are plenty of books already out there on that), it is imperative to have some basics under your belt.

This chapter will give you a kickstart of some fundamental PowerShell knowledge and go over the common cmdlets that you will use when implementing the deployment template for both simple and complex deployments.

If you are already fairly good at PowerShell, you can go ahead and skip right over to the next chapter. If not, stick with it and by the end, everything else in the following chapters will be straightforward as you'll have a clear understanding of what you are looking at and of the template itself.

There's a lot of ground to cover here, even if it is a crash course. As Lao Tzu once said, *"A journey of a thousand miles begins with a single step."*

Writing Code

You do not need to write PowerShell in any special editor although it's certainly advisable. You can just as easily write your code in any text editor such as the built-in Windows Notepad as you could in Visual Studio Code, VSCode, or any other of the hundreds of coding applications currently available.

© Owen Heaume 2022
O. Heaume, *Understanding Microsoft Intune*,
https://doi.org/10.1007/978-1-4842-8850-4_1

The PowerShell template used in this book does not need advanced features such as GitHub integration or advanced debugging offered in more complicated solutions. Therefore, I recommend that you use the PowerShell ISE (Integrated Scripting Environment) that is built right into Windows when first starting out; it's simple, clean, and forgoes an overwhelming learning curve.

If you are already comfortable using a third-party ISE, then go ahead and use it. For this book though, the built-in PowerShell ISE will be used, and you can launch it by opening the Run command dialog box using the keyboard shortcut combination of **Windows key + R** and typing in **powershell ise**. (See Figure 1-1) This will launch the PowerShell ISE nonelevated.

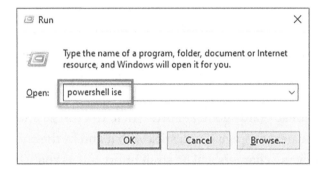

Figure 1-1. *Launching PowerShell ISE from the Run dialog*

It is within the ISE that you will write and test the PowerShell code for the deployment template.

It's simple to use too. Let's try a quick example.

Type the following in the scripting window (white space area) within the ISE:

```
Write-Host "Isn't this fun?"
```

Execute the code by clicking the green arrow in the toolbar. The code executes and the results are displayed in the blue console window at the bottom. (See Figure 1-2)

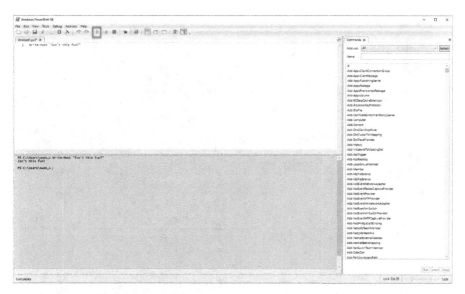

Figure 1-2. *The PowerShell ISE*

Tip   Hover your mouse over any toolbar button to see a brief tooltip about each one. For instance, if you hover your mouse over the green arrow button that you just clicked, it tells you that you can also press F5 on your keyboard to execute the code. Now that's handy!

The blue window in the bottom pane of the ISE is known as the console, and not only will it display the results of your code execution from the scripting window, but you are also able to type directly into it and press enter on your keyboard to execute its contents.

You can also launch either the PowerShell ISE or console by typing **powershell** in the Windows search bar located in the taskbar where you will then be presented with further options to run PowerShell Console or PowerShell ISE as Administrator. (This may be required when using PowerShell cmdlets that require elevation privileges.) (See Figure 1-3)

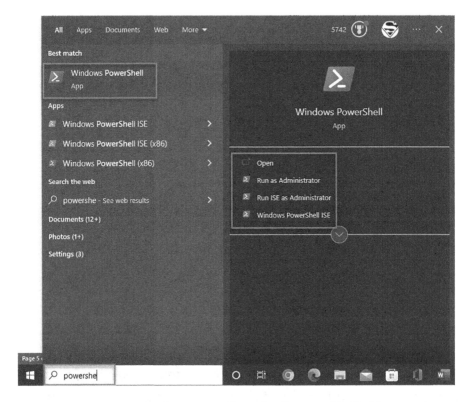

Figure 1-3. *Using Windows search to find PowerShell. Note options to run PowerShell or the ISE as Administrator*

PowerShell Cmdlets

Cmdlets (pronounced command-lets) are native PowerShell commands. They always follow the same naming convention of *verb-noun*. For example, get-process.

Cmdlets usually do one thing and one thing only. As a result, there are thousands of PowerShell cmdlets available across a range of providers. (PowerShell providers are .NET programs that provide access to specialized data stores, for example, the file system or the registry. The data appears in a drive, and you access the data in a path like you would on a hard disk drive.)

Try typing the following directly into the blue console window in your ISE to see the available cmdlets installed on your computer:

```
Get-Command
```

You can also type **powershell** in the Run menu to open a separate instance of just the PowerShell console. (See Figure 1-4)

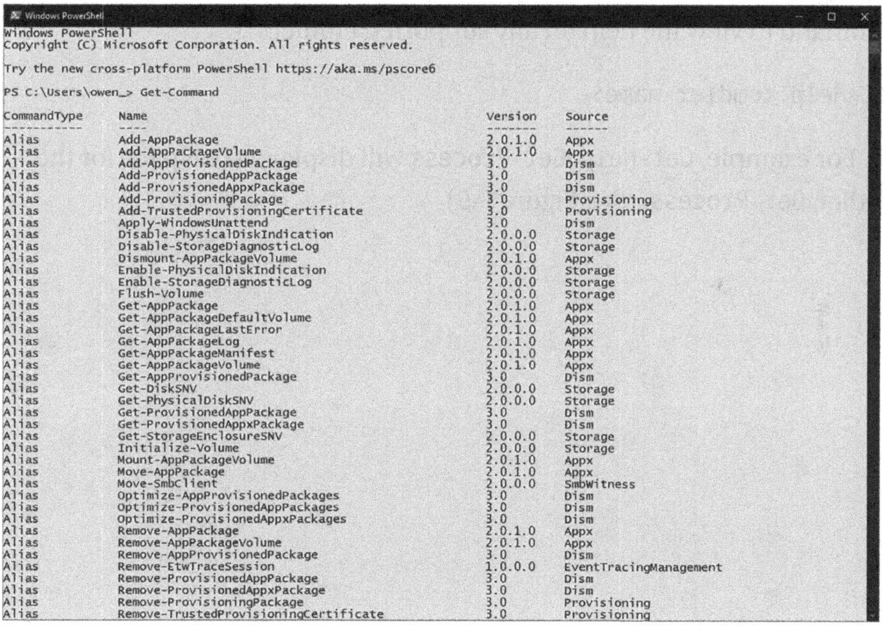

Figure 1-4. *The results of Get-Command are shown in a separate instance of the PowerShell Console*

On my computer, I have over 1600 cmdlets available to use. Phew!

It's Okay to Ask for Help

With that many cmdlets available, you may be thinking about how you can remember them all and any parameters they may accept.

Luckily, the PowerShell team created help files for most of them and the first thing to do is to update the help files on your computer if you haven't already done so.

In the PowerShell console (either stand-alone or the console within the ISE), type and execute the following to update the help files:

```
Update-Help
```

It may take a few moments to run depending on the speed of your Internet connection. Once it's updated you can run the following command to view the help on any supported cmdlet:

```
Get-Help <cmdlet name>
```

For example, `Get-Help Get-Process` will display the help file for the cmdlet, `Get-Process`. (See Figure 1-5)

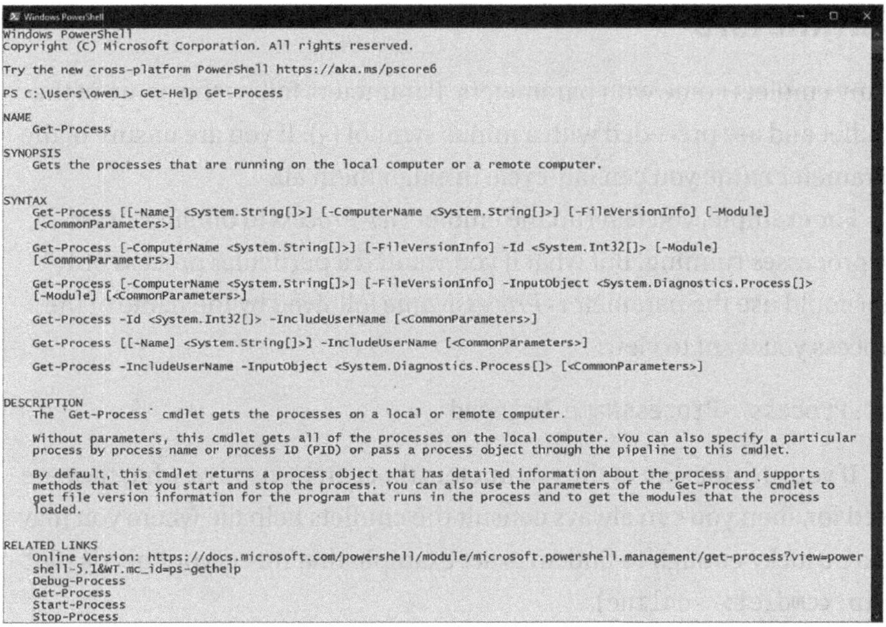

Figure 1-5. *The help file for Get-Process*

You can also add parameters to enhance the help offered. Try:

```
Get-Help <cmdlet> -Full
```

or:

```
Get-Help <cmdlet> -ShowWindow.
```

Or my personal favorite:

```
Get-Help <cmdlet> -Online
```

You can even run Get-Help on itself! Try:

```
Get-Help Get-Help
```

Parameters

Many cmdlets come with parameters. Parameters follow the name of the cmdlet and are preceded with a minus symbol (-). If you are unsure of the parameter name you can tab-cycle through them all.

For example, you can run the cmdlet *Get-Process* to obtain a list of *all* processes running. But what if you wanted a particular process only? You could use the parameter *-ProcessName* followed by the name of the process you want to view:

```
Get-Process -ProcessName Notepad
```

If you are not sure of the parameters that can be used or what they are used for, then you can always consult the cmdlets help file where you may also be lucky enough to find an exact example that meets your needs (`Get-Help <cmdlet> -online`).

Pipeline

The output of one cmdlet can be used as the input of another. This works from left to right and the pipe symbol is used to send the results of the preceding command to the next command. For example (and please do not run this example for real), the output of *Get-Process* can be used as the input for *Stop-Process*:

```
Get-Process | Stop-Process
```

On my UK English keyboard, the pipe symbol is found by pressing SHIFT + backslash (the key to the immediate left of "z").

The Ten Cmdlets

In the sea of cmdlets available, you may feel like you are drowning. Let me throw you a lifejacket then and reveal that you only need to understand ten cmdlets for deploying most applications that come your way.

The following cmdlets should be understood thoroughly before continuing with the rest of the book. Make yourself a cup of tea or coffee and take a moment to try each of them in a PowerShell session and invest some time looking at the relevant help files. I recommend using online help (Get-Help <cmdlet> -online).

Write-Host

This cmdlet's primary purpose is to provide output to the screen. It can also color text output by supplying the **-ForegroundColor** parameter as shown in Figure 1-6.

Windows PowerShell
```
Windows PowerShell
Copyright (C) Microsoft Corporation. All rights reserved.

Try the new cross-platform PowerShell https://aka.ms/pscore6

PS C:\Users\owen_> Write-Host "This sentence is in green!" -ForegroundColor Green
This sentence is in green!
PS C:\Users\owen_>
```

Figure 1-6. *Write-Host can also display text in color*

However, ***Write-Host*** can also be used to inform Intune whether something in the deployment template ran successfully or not. You will see later in the book how this works. In its Intune context, it is quite often used within a ***Try/Catch*** block.

Get-Location/Set-Location

Get-Location will get the current working location. For example, *C:\myFiles* as shown in Figure 1-7.

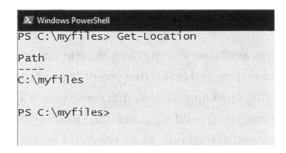

Figure 1-7. *Get-Location displays the current working directory*

You can recall the path for later use by assigning it to a variable. In PowerShell, variables are preceded with the dollar ($) symbol. The name of the variable can be almost anything you like.

The following code assigns the current working location to a variable named $myPath:

```
$myPath = Get-Location
```

Set-Location is its big brother (or sister). This command will *set* the working location to the one you have defined in the parameter **-Path**

Figure 1-8 shows that the working location was originally *C:\MyFiles* and by using *Set-Location* the working location changed to *C:\Temp*.

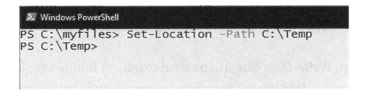

Figure 1-8. *Set-Location has changed the current working directory to C:\Temp*

Get-Process

Get-Process will get a list of all running processes on a local or remote computer. (See Figure 1-9)

```
Windows PowerShell
PS C:\Temp> Get-Process

Handles  NPM(K)     PM(K)     WS(K)    CPU(s)      Id  SI ProcessName
-------  ------     -----     -----    ------      --  -- -----------
    287      17      4952     25336      0.38   12400   1 ApplicationFrame
    347      17    140440    182248      6.31    2108   1 chrome
    227      15     19336     32488      0.11    4644   1 chrome
    232      15      7080     17872      0.06    6692   1 chrome
    487      21    168528    220204     50.95    6876   1 chrome
   1425      49    123848    210988     37.59    9064   1 chrome
    208      13      8000     18280      0.27    9140   1 chrome
    331      24     18040     42872      7.56   10672   1 chrome
    165       9      1932      7420      0.05   13240   1 chrome
    430      27     98232     90676      5.36   13260   1 chrome
    102       7      6240     10128               4584   0 conhost
    102       7      6344      1084      0.08   10344   1 conhost
    230      13      4260     15848      3.09   12332   1 conhost
```

Figure 1-9. *Get-Process: you can see the process name column on the right*

You may have an application that will not install if a certain process is running. In a deployment scenario, *Get-Process* can test that the process is running first, before piping (sending) it to *Stop-Process*.

Stop-Process

Stop-Process will stop all instances of a running process.

Say you had an application that would not install if Notepad was running; you could add a prerequisite in the deployment template (more on this later) to test for the running process and if found, stop it.

Try this: open Notepad on your computer, and then type the following and observe the result:

```
Stop-Process -ProcessName "notepad"
```

By default, *Stop-Process* will stop any process owned by the current user.

If the process is not owned by the current user and the command is not being run with administrative privileges, then an access denied message is displayed.

11

If the process is not owned by the current user but the command is run with administrative privileges then a prompt is displayed asking if you are sure you wish to perform the action, and then awaits a keypress to either confirm or deny the action; certainly not the desired outcome when deploying scripts. (See Figure 1-10)

```
Administrator: Windows PowerShell
Windows PowerShell
Copyright (C) Microsoft Corporation. All rights reserved.

Try the new cross-platform PowerShell https://aka.ms/pscore6

PS C:\WINDOWS\system32> Stop-Process -ProcessName lsass

Confirm
Are you sure you want to perform the Stop-Process operation on the following item: lsass(632)?
[Y] Yes  [A] Yes to All  [N] No  [L] No to All  [S] Suspend  [?] Help (default is "Y"):
```

Figure 1-10. *Note the PowerShell console title bar shows it is running with administrative privileges. This now causes a confirmation prompt before the action is executed*

To avoid this undesired confirmation prompt, and I've been building up to this moment since starting to write the chapter, you will need to use The Force!

By adding the -**Force** parameter, the desired process will end without question:

   Stop-Process -ProcessName "lsass" -Force

Start-Process

Start-Process is an easy cmdlet to grasp because it simply starts a process on a local computer.

There's a lot more to *Start-Process* than meets the eye though and you will be reading more about this cmdlet in a later chapter.

It's an easy cmdlet to demonstrate so try this in your PowerShell console:

```
Start-Process -FilePath "c:\windows\system32\notepad.exe"
```

New-Item

New-Item creates a new item and can also set its value. The type of item it creates depends on the location. For instance, in the file system, it can create files and folders; however, in the registry, it will create registry keys and entries.

This cmdlet shines in deployments and is particularly useful for custom detection rules. (More of this later in the book.)

In this example, a text file is created named testfile.txt in the directory c:\myfiles. Additionally, the text file has the text "This is a text string." (See Figure 1-11)

Figure 1-11. *Creating a new text file containing text*

Try this for yourself, ensuring that the path you select exists first.

```
New-Item -Path "c:\myfiles" -Name "testfile.txt" -ItemType
"file" -Value "This is a text string."
```

New-ItemProperty

This cmdlet is mainly used for creating a new item and setting its value. It is typically used to create new registry values.

13

In the context of deploying applications, this is frequently used for custom detection scripts or simply manipulating the registry as part of a pre- or post-application deployment.

In a later chapter, you will study this cmdlet in more detail so for now, look at the help file and familiarize yourself with some of the examples given in the documentation:

```
Get-Help New-ItemProperty -Online
```

Get-Item

This cmdlet gets an item and is very flexible in what it can do. Frequently used in detection rules, it can effortlessly obtain a version number from an executable, which can then be used to compare against an expected value.

Figure 1-12 shows how to obtain the version number of snagit.exe.

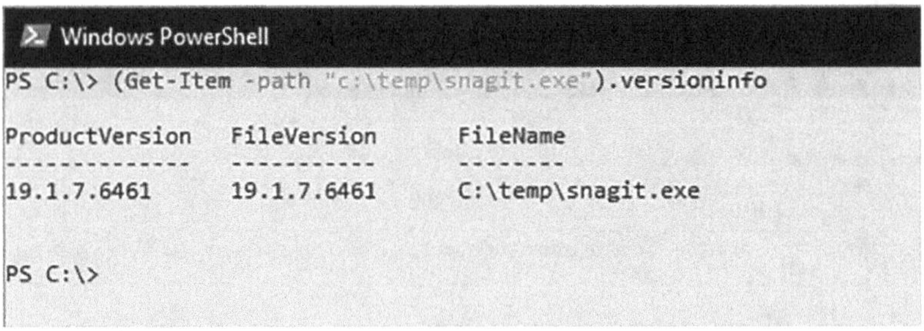

Figure 1-12. *Obtaining the version number of an executable*

You will learn more about this cmdlet in a later chapter.

Copy-Item

Copy-Item is useful for copying items in the same namespace from one location to another. For instance, copying files to a folder. It's self-explanatory to use – this example copies a text file to the *MyFiles* Directory:

```
Copy-Item -Path "C:\temp\A Text Document.txt" -Destination
"C:\MyFiles"
```

Test-Path

This cmdlet is used to determine if a file or folder in a given path exists or not. If the path exists it returns true, if not it returns false.

Figure 1-13 demonstrates using *Test-Path* to determine if the file "*A text document.txt*" exists in *C:\Temp*. The cmdlet returns true – the file exists!

```
Test-Path -Path "C:\temp\A Text Document.txt"
```

Figure 1-13. *True has been returned signifying "C:\temp\A text Document.txt" exists*

The more astute among you may have noticed that I paired the two cmdlets: *Get-Location* with *Set-Location*. I'll hold my hands up; you caught me. Technically it's eleven cmdlets but I wanted to use the whole *The Ten Cmdlets* heading thing as a play on words, so what's a guy supposed to do?

Warning   If a cmdlet begins with the verb **get-** then it will perform a nondestructive read-only operation. Be careful to test any cmdlet beginning with the verb **set- (or other PowerShell verbs you may not be familiar with)**, as this operation could make destructive changes and may have undesired effects if used improperly.

While there are only a few cmdlets to learn, they should cover about 99% of any complex or odd deployment requests that come your way. For that edge-case 1% that lands on your table: you are now fully equipped on how to read the help for the cmdlets that you have yet to discover.

Scripting

As said earlier, this book was never about teaching PowerShell or scripting. Its purpose is to provide you with an easy-to-use template that enables you to deploy simple or complicated applications in a reliable and repeatable way using Microsoft Intune. Having said that, it would be remiss of me if I didn't provide a bit of help in the world of scripting; at least in the context of the deployment template that you are working towards.

There's a lot to learn when it comes to scripting and, although this book is not about to turn you into the next scripting master, it may be helpful to go over a few basic constructs.

What About That Help?

PowerShell comes with many constructs that can help with scripting, for example, Do, While, and For loops or functions and advanced functions, variables, etc. So how do you look up help for these topics?

In the PowerShell Console or ISE console, type the following for a list of topics that you can obtain help about:

```
help about
```

(See Figure 1-14)

```
Windows PowerShell
PS C:\Users\owen_> help about

Name                              Category  Module
----                              --------  ------
about_Aliases                     HelpFile
about_Alias_Provider              HelpFile
about_Arithmetic_Operators        HelpFile
about_Arrays                      HelpFile
about_Assignment_Operators        HelpFile
about_Automatic_Variables         HelpFile
about_Booleans                    HelpFile
about_Break                       HelpFile
about_Built-in_Functions          HelpFile
about_Calculated_Properties       HelpFile
about_Case-Sensitivity            HelpFile
about_Certificate_Provider        HelpFile
```

Figure 1-14. *A list of help topics is displayed*

To view help about a specific topic, for example, Booleans, type the following in the PowerShell Console:

Help about_booleans

(See Figure 1-15)

```
Windows PowerShell
PS C:\Users\owen_> help about_booleans

ABOUT_BOOLEANS


PowerShell can implicitly treat any type as a BOOLEAN. It is important to
understand the rules that PowerShell uses to convert other types to BOOLEAN
values.


Converting from scalar types

A scalar type is an atomic quantity that can hold only one value at a time.
The following types evaluate to $false:

-    Empty strings like '' or ""
-    Null values like $null
-    Any numeric type with the value of 0

Examples:

    PS> $false -eq ''
    True
    PS> if ("") { $true } else { $false }
```

Figure 1-15. *The help topic about booleans is displayed*

Try/Catch/Finally

Try/Catch block is great for trapping potential errors and taking alternative action if an error is detected. It can be explained something like this: "*Try and perform the following commands, but if it doesn't work, catch the error and do this instead.*"

In the following example code, it tries to do something with the word "error" in the *try* block, but as PowerShell does not know what this is it will generate an error.

Because an error was caused, the *catch* block takes effect, and a message is displayed to the user informing them that there was an error.

The optional *Finally* block will always run regardless of an error being produced or not.

Try/Catch/Finally

```
try {
    # this will produce an error
    error
} catch {
    # Catch any error that occurred
    Write-host "An error occurred!" -ForegroundColor DarkRed
} finally {
    # Clean up code
    write-host "This part will always run."
    -ForegroundColor Cyan
}
```

There are many facets to a Try/Catch/Finally block, and I urge you to explore the help documentation:

```
Help about_Try_Catch_Finally
```

If/Else

The If statement is used a great deal in scripting. It's used in a manner akin to this: "*If* this condition is met then do this, otherwise (or *else*) do this instead."

Note the "*Else*" is optional – you can use *If* by itself if that is all it takes to achieve your goal.

Here's an example where you might use an *If/Else*: let's say you wanted to copy files to a destination directory *C:\Destination* but only if the destination directory already existed. If the destination directory did not exist, you would take some other action; perhaps create the directory first and then copy the file.

You know from studying the previous cmdlets that *Test-Path* will result in either true or false depending on if the specified path exists or not. In this scenario, it's the perfect cmdlet to use with the If statement.

By default, If will recognize a true response on the condition between the brackets and execute the code to copy files without you having to explicitly state "if test-path returns true."

However, if *Test-Path* returns false (the path does not exist), then the code in the *else* block will execute instead.

If: Will copy files if Test-Path returns true, otherwise it will create the directory first and then copy files.

```
If (Test-path c:\destination) {
    # Copy some files!
} else {
    # 1. Create the directory as it does not exist.
    # 2. Now copy the files.
}
```

If you wanted to test for a false response you can use an exclamation mark. This reverses the evaluation: "*If* Test-Path returns false then do this, otherwise (*else*) do this."

If: Reversing the evaluation using an exclamation mark. Now If Test-Path does not exist, create the directory and then copy files.

```
If (!(Test-path c:\destination)) {
    # 1. Create the directory as it does not exist.
    # 2. Now copy the files.
} else {
    # Copy some files!
}
```

Once again, I urge you to view the help topic on this:

```
Help about_if
```

Summary

That was a tough chapter, and if you were new to PowerShell then you will now have a solid grounding not only for the rest of this book but also for using PowerShell in general.

You have learned about cmdlets and how to get help, parameters, and pipelines and which ten (ahem!) cmdlets to study that will give you a head start into application deployment.

You then had a brief overview of PowerShell scripting and discovered the "help about" topics to prepare for the way ahead.

In the next chapter, you will learn some more fundamentals on using the built-in tool MSIEXEC.exe as well as exploring some advanced MSI techniques.

CHAPTER 2

MSIEXEC

Msiexec.exe provides the means to install, modify, and perform operations on Windows Installer from the command line. This is the tool that, where possible, you should try to use all the time to install applications.

Msiexec can install MSI and MSP (patches) as well as accept parameters and MST (transform) files to customize the deployment.

It's the easiest "tool" to use to deploy MSI files because it just works, and it provides the greatest flexibility.

It is another crucial step to master if you are to become a deployment expert and, in this chapter, you will learn about the relevant parameters it can accept, how to find valid property values and uninstall GUIDS.

Fundamentals

Msiexec.exe is found natively on all modern Microsoft Windows operating systems today. It is used to install applications that are in the MSI format. Any application that has the *.msi* extension can be double-clicked and *msiexe.exe* will launch automatically to install it.

View the Help

Msiexec.exe has a lot of parameters that can be passed to it, and you will learn about the pertinent ones later in this chapter. To view the available parameters, you can read the help that comes bundled with the tool.

© Owen Heaume 2022
O. Heaume, *Understanding Microsoft Intune*,
https://doi.org/10.1007/978-1-4842-8850-4_2

Begin by opening the Run menu and typing in `msiexec /?`. (See Figure 2-1)

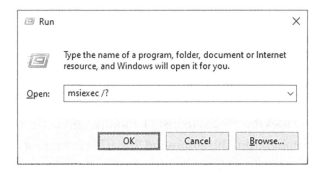

Figure 2-1. *Launching the msiexec help from the Run dialog*

Once you click the OK button, the help is displayed as shown in Figure 2-2.

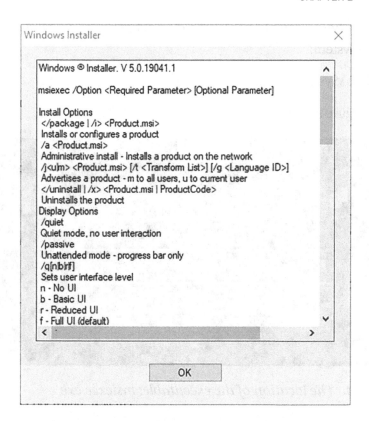

Figure 2-2. *The msiexec help file*

This help file is useful for a quick reminder when you are on the go. Should you want more detailed help you should read the online help and I recommend taking a five-minute break to read through it.

The online documentation can be read here: *https://docs. microsoft.com/en-gb/windows/win32/msi/command-line-options*

Where Is It?

As you've just been shown, when you type *msiexec /?* directly into the Run dialog, it will automatically launch; you don't need to type the complete file path to call it. For clarity and certainty, you should use the full path to msiexec.exe's location when using it in PowerShell scripts.

Here's where it can be found if the drive letter C: contains the operating system:

`C:\Windows\System32`

(See Figure 2-3)

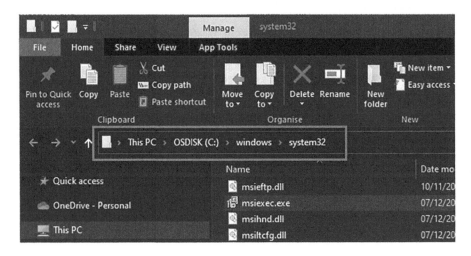

Figure 2-3. *The location of the executable: msiexec.exe*

Reference msiexec by using the full path:

`C:\Windows\System32\msiexc.exe`

Better to Use $Env:

"Better to use say what?" Yup, as you have just read, when accessing msiexec by using the full path, you are assuming that Windows was installed and accessed via the drive letter of C: But what if Windows was installed on drive D: or E: or any other drive letter?

If a PowerShell script has been hard coded to reference msiexec from C:\Windows\System32 and Windows was installed on "D:", then the deployment script would fail.

So how do you work around this issue? PowerShell includes many environment variables which come to the rescue for just such a situation.

Environment variables store data that is used by the operating system and other programs. Some hold paths (as you will shortly learn) while others may hold data about the logged-in user. (More on this later.)

There are many environment variables, and your PowerShell scripts can query them to determine the value.

In the PowerShell ISE, if you begin to type $ENV: the IntelliSense will display the available environment variables. (See Figure 2-4)

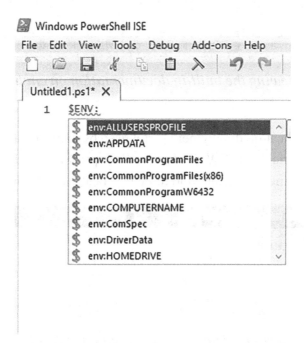

Figure 2-4. *PowerShell IntelliSense: Just start typing $ENV:*

You can also read all about PowerShell environment variables by typing:

`help about_Environment_Variables` in the PowerShell console. (See Figure 2-5)

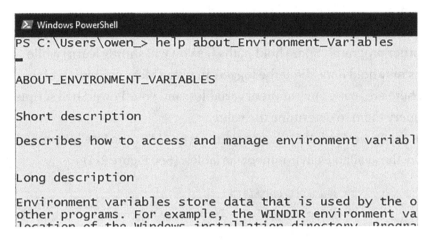

Figure 2-5. *Viewing the built-in documentation on environment variables*

For the application deployment script used by this book, the environment variable of `$ENV:SystemRoot` is appropriate as this will always resolve to the Windows installation directory. Figure 2-6 demonstrates this.

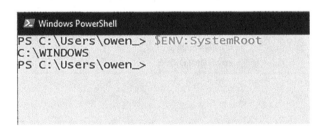

Figure 2-6. *The value of $ENV:SystemRoot is C:\Windows on this computer*

With that in mind, you should always reference any calls to msiexec. exe in your deployment scripts using the PowerShell environment variable:

```
$ENV:SystemRoot\System32\msiexec.exe
```

Even if you are certain that you will be deploying to computers that have a standard Windows installation using the drive letter "C:", it is very good practice to get into the habit of using environment variables wherever possible. After all, you may write a script for yourself now that you end up sharing later and who knows where the Windows installation resides in another organization?

Parameters

Before you begin your journey in earnest, you must understand the fundamentals of building up a command line to either install or uninstall an MSI application using msiexec.exe.

The parameters that you will mostly use with msiexec are /i , /x, /qn, / norestart, and sometimes PROPERTY.

I never find myself using the TRANSFORMS switch though there are certainly great use-cases for it and once again it's worth a time-out to read the online documentation referenced earlier (if you haven't already done so) to understand when a transforms file may be worth your while.

It is beyond the scope of this book to walk you through every single option available, so you will learn about the parameters used in most deployments. Let's see how to build up a typical command line to install a fictitious MSI application: *MyProduct.msi*.

Installation

To install an MSI use the /i as your first switch followed by your .msi file:

```
msiexec /i MyProduct.msi
```

Silent Install

To make this installation silent, that is, no GUI or user interaction displayed, add /qn:

```
msiexec /i MyProduct.msi /qn
```

No Restart

The install must not restart the computer that you deploy the MSI to as there may be post-deployment tasks to complete; suppress the restart by adding /norestart

```
 msiexec /i MyProduct.msi /qn /norestart
```

Uninstall

Uninstalling is a similar process, except /x instead of /i as the first parameter.

This example shows the command line for silent uninstall and suppresses any restarts:

```
msiexec /x MyProduct.msi /qn /norestart
```

At this stage, you cannot simply type: msiexec /i MyProduct.msi /qn /norestart (or any other msiexec command line) in the PowerShell deployment script and expect it to work – It still requires some PowerShell magic to make it function correctly. This is covered later in the book.

That's essentially it for parameters. Of course, there are other parameters you can use as you saw from looking at the help, but these are the common ones that you will find yourself using in deployment scenarios.

Now that you have the basics under your belt, when it comes to scripting this later it will be a breeze.

Properties

Some MSIs have properties you can modify to customize the installation. For example, automatically accepting an End User License Agreement (EULA) or preventing the creation of a desktop shortcut. You do this by referencing the property with the associated value when you create your command line.

`msiexec /i MyProduct.msi PROPERTY=value /qn /norestart` where PROPERTY is the name of the property you wish to modify, and value is the value for that property.

You may or may not already know what the properties and values are that you require for your command line. On very rare occasions a product will come with some great documentation, and you know ahead of time exactly what you need.

But what if you don't know this information? How can you find out which properties are available and what the permitted values are for them?

Which Properties Can Be Set?

There is more than one way to find out which properties can be configured for a given MSI, and the easiest method, as it does not require any extra "tools," is to add some logging parameters to the install command line, and then perform a manual install on a test computer.

By examining the resulting log output, you can view which properties are available.

Enable logging using the /lp! switch followed by the name of the log file:

```
msiexec /i <msi_name> /lp! <msi_property_logfile>
```

You can name the MSI property logfile anything you like, for example:

```
msiexec /i MyProgram.msi /lp! PropertyLog.txt
```

Once you have installed the MSI with logging turned on, look at the resulting: PropertyLog.txt: any Property(S) or Property(C) in the log that is in capitals is a public property and can usually be configured.

Figure 2-7 is the resulting log file of an MSI install and shows the property **ERPSYSTEM** can be configured as part of the installation if desired. By default, it has a value of *Sage1000*.

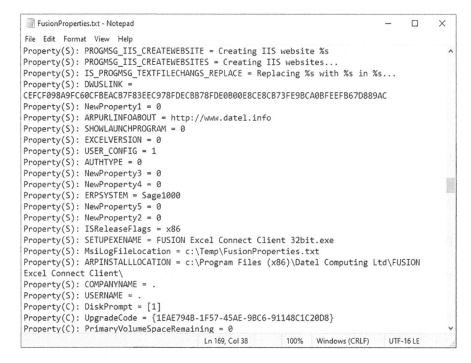

Figure 2-7. *ERPSYSTEM is a public property and can be configured as part of the MSI installation*

How to Find Valid Property Values

Understanding how to determine which properties may be modified as part of an MSI installation is a useful skill; however, on many an occasion, you will not know what the permitted property values are.

Finding out what these are is a straightforward process. You do this by installing the MSI first on a test computer having added the logging parameter to the installation command line.

Once you have manually selected all the desired install options, allow the installation to complete and inspect the resulting log file.

Let's have an example: you must deploy an application, *FUSION Excel Connect Client 32bit.msi*, that requires user input to change a default configuration.

Figure 2-8 shows that manually executing the MSI displays a default value of *Sage 1000* for the ERP System. The company requires this setting to be changed to *Sage Enterprise Management*.

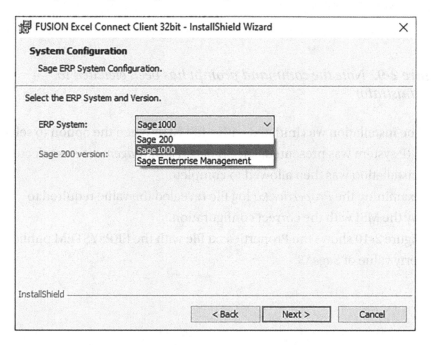

Figure 2-8. *ERPSYSTEM needs to be changed from Sage 1000 to Sage Enterprise Management*

Using the previously shown technique to view the available properties from the log file, it was seen that the property to be set is ERPSYSTEM, but what should the correct property value be?

To find out, install the MSI with logging turned on using the following command line:

```
msiexec /i "FUSION Excel Connect Client 32bit.msi" /lp!
PropertyLog.txt
```

Remember to use an administrative command prompt when installing. (See Figure 2-9)

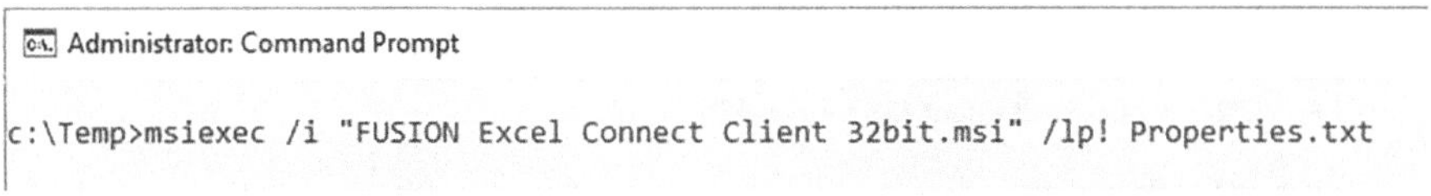

Figure 2-9. *Note the command prompt has been elevated to Administrator*

The installation was initiated with a full GUI. When the option to select the ERP system was presented, *Sage Enterprise Management* was selected. The installation was then allowed to complete.

Examining the *Properties.txt* log file revealed the value required to deploy the MSI with the correct configuration.

Figure 2-10 shows the Properties.txt file with the ERPSYSTEM public property value of *SageX3*.

Figure 2-10. The property value for the desired setting change is SageX3

Armed with this knowledge, to successfully *install "Fusion Excel Connect Client 32bit.msi"* silently, suppressing any reboots and changing the default configuration to *Sage Enterprise Management,* the installation command line would now be:

```
msiexec /i "FUSION Excel Connect Client 32bit.msi"
ERPSYSTEM=SageX3 /qn /norestart
```

Uninstall GUIDs

There may come a time when you are required to uninstall an MSI before installing a new version.

When you install an MSI, it stores various useful information, including its display name and uninstall GUID in the registry.

Where this useful information is stored depends on whether it was a 32-bit or 64-bit installation.

32-Bit Installations

Here is the location in the registry for 32-bit installations:

```
HKLM:\SOFTWARE\Wow6432Node\Microsoft\Windows\CurrentVersion\
Uninstall
```

You will need to have a click-around on the various GUID subkeys to find the application you are looking for.

Figure 2-11 displays the details for the 32-bit installation of the Fusion Connect Client and reveals a lot of useful application information.

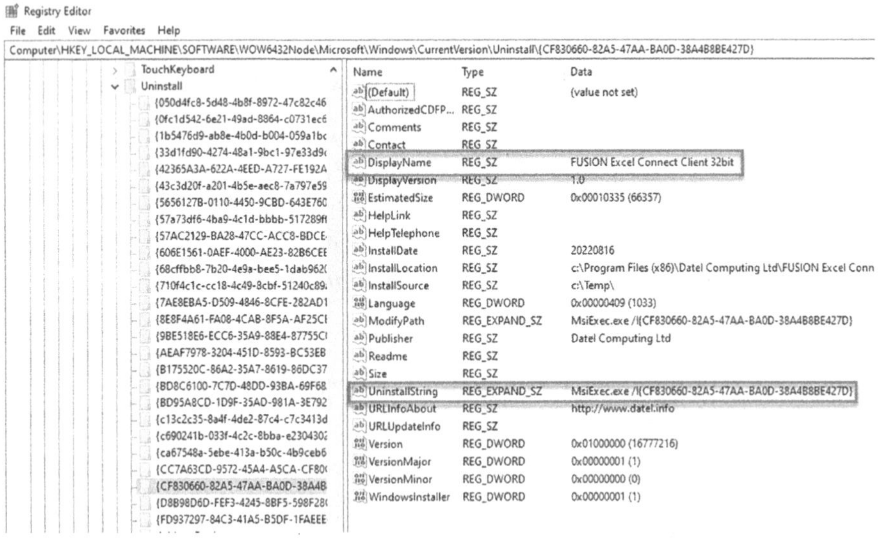

Figure 2-11. *Inspecting the application information in the registry for 32-bit installations*

The most important registry values (as far as scripting an uninstall goes) are the *Display Name* and *Uninstall String*, as with these two pieces of information you can easily test for and script the uninstallation of a particular application.

To uninstall an MSI using the discovered uninstall string you use the /x switch followed by the GUID enclosed in the curly braces:

```
Msiexec /x {CF830660-82A5-47AA-BA0D-38A4B8BE427D}
```

Msiexec.exe allows you to uninstall silently and suppress reboots by using the same switches as previously explained:

```
Msiexec /x {CF830660-82A5-47AA-BA0D-38A4B8BE427D} /
norestart /qn
```

Tip   The Wow6432Node registry entry indicates that you are running a 64-bit Windows version. The operating system uses this key to display a separate view of HKEY_LOCAL_MACHINE\SOFTWARE for 32-bit applications that run on 64-bit Windows versions.

64-Bit Installations

The uninstall registry location for 64-bit MSIs can be found at

```
HKLM:\SOFTWARE\Microsoft\Windows\CurrentVersion\Uninstall
```

And here are the details for the 64-bit version of the same program. As you can see, the same application information is presented. (See Figure 2-12)

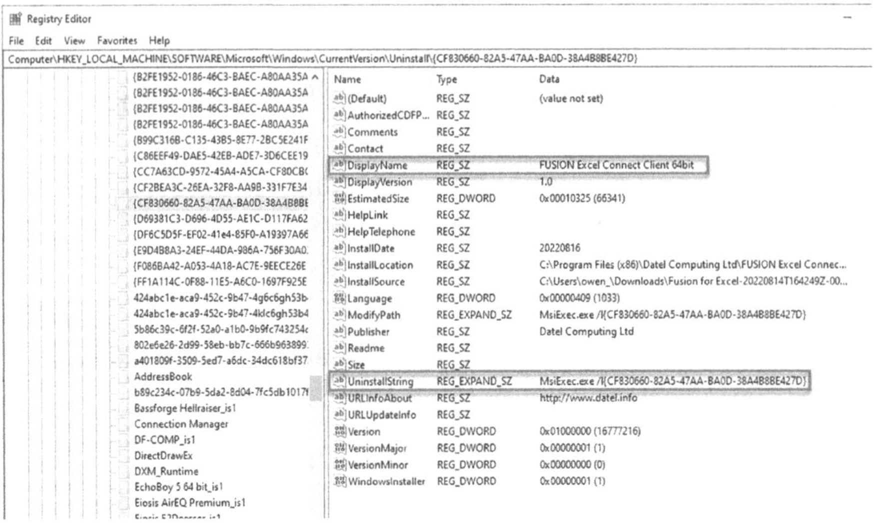

Figure 2-12. *The 64-bit uninstall location in the registry*

Knowing where to find the uninstall information enables you to search for the display name of the application that you wish to uninstall. You can then obtain the corresponding uninstall GUID before passing it to msiexec. exe to begin the uninstallation.

Tip   If there is a chance that some computers may have older versions of the software you are about to deploy, it's best to verify if an older installed version exists first, and if so, uninstall it before the new application is installed. Now I don't know about you, but that sounds like it would be an ideal candidate for a pre-deployment task that can be handled by a deployment template. Later in the book, it will be explained how to handle this exact scenario.

This was another heavy chapter, but like the chapter before, crucial to understand if you are to become a deployment guru.

Summary

In this chapter, you learned that MSIEXE.exe has built-in help files as well as a superior online help document, why it's better to use PowerShell environment variables rather than hard-coding a path, and the various parameters that are used with most scripted application deployments.

You learned that you could customize the MSI installation by setting properties, how to view the allowed properties, and how to discover the valid property values.

You finished up by learning about the uninstall information that is written to the registry on every MSI installation.

The next chapter focuses on how to approach the dreaded Setup.exe.

CHAPTER 3

Setup.exe

Any administrator will relate to the dread of receiving an application that arrives as a setup.exe file. Notoriously difficult and sometimes seemingly impossible to deploy, they often arrive with little or no help files.

There are a few techniques that you can employ to help mitigate some of the anxiety a setup.exe can bring, and this chapter will cover the tried-and-tested ones that I have employed during my years of application deployment.

Discovering the Setup.exe Silent Install/Uninstall Parameters

A silent installation or uninstallation of any application is imperative when deploying to end users when using Intune. Finding the silent install and uninstall command line switches for these can be tricky. Here are a few techniques to try if you've not had any luck with the (rarely) supplied documentation.

EXEs Have Registry Information Too

It's worth pointing out that you won't just find MSI installation information at the 32-bit and 64-bit registry uninstall subkeys (as you learned in the previous chapter), you will also find information on setup.exe.

If you are lucky, the supplier of the application may include the exact command line in the registry, required for silent uninstall too as shown in Figure 3-1.

© Owen Heaume 2022

O. Heaume, *Understanding Microsoft Intune*,

https://doi.org/10.1007/978-1-4842-8850-4_3

MajorVersion	REG_DWORD	0x000007e6 (2022)
MinorVersion	REG_DWORD	0x00000006 (6)
NoModify	REG_DWORD	0x00000001 (1)
NoRepair	REG_DWORD	0x00000001 (1)
Publisher	REG_SZ	Kilohearts AB
QuietUninstallString	REG_SZ	"C:\ProgramData\Kilohearts\unins000.exe" /SILENT
UninstallString	REG_SZ	"C:\ProgramData\Kilohearts\unins000.exe"
URLInfoAbout	REG_SZ	https://www.kilohearts.com/
VersionMajor	REG_DWORD	0x000007e6 (2022)
VersionMinor	REG_DWORD	0x00000006 (6)

Figure 3-1. *A lucky find! Querying the registry for the uninstall string*

In-Built Help

Typing: setup.exe /? (You may need to replace the word 'setup' with the application name if it is named differently) at a command prompt may provide you with the command line switches you are going to need. Make sure that you are in the same working directory as the setup.exe file when you do this. (See Figure 3-2)

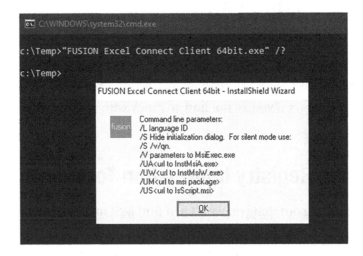

Figure 3-2. *A setup.exe displaying help – a rare find indeed*

Internet Search

There's no shame in throwing your hands in the air and having to search the Internet for the information you need. You may discover a blog where someone has figured this all out for you already, and there is certainly no need to reinvent the wheel.

On many an occasion, I have found what I need by visiting the official website of the application I was trying to deploy; often there is install advice for admins and sometimes an MSI alternative to download. Failing that, it's always worth reaching out to their technical support email or phone number to see if they can help; I have had success using this method on rare occasions.

MSI Extraction

Sometimes it's downright impossible to obtain or figure out the silent uninstall command line switches for a setup.exe. It's always preferable to deploy an MSI and therefore another technique to try in this situation is MSI extraction.

Some, but not all, setup.exe files are wrappers for MSI files, and it may be possible to extract the MSI from them.

MSI Extraction Method #1

This is the quickest of the two extraction methods. Try to extract the MSI from setup.exe using a program like 7-Zip. (Right-click the setup.exe and select one of the "Extract" options.) The resulting extraction may provide you with the required MSI file. Figure 3-3 shows an attempted MSI extraction using 7-Zip.

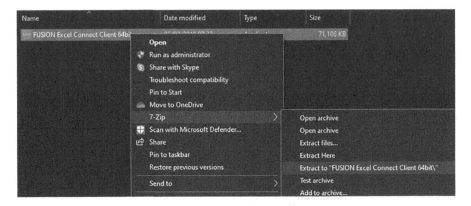

Figure 3-3. *Attempting to extract an MSI using 7-Zip*

MSI Extraction Method #2

This technique can work well and is worth your time trying. Many setup programs extract their contents to a temporary location first, and in some cases, the extracted contents may include an MSI.

To use this extraction technique, manually install the program but just before you click "Next" to commence the install, browse to the *%temp%* directory (in the Run menu type %temp%), and locate the folder that contains the program extracted files.

Once you have done that, if present, copy the MSI to another location before you cancel the manual install process you started.

This method always worked well on Java runtime executables (JRE) which for many now, along with Adobe Flash, are thankfully a deployment of the past.

Tip   You learned in Chapter 1 that when scripting paths it was better to use PowerShell's environment variables; these environment variables always resolve to specific locations. Windows also has environment variables, and you access them by surrounding the variable name with a percentage symbol (%). The example you just saw in *MSI Extraction Method #2* uses the *%temp%* environment variable which will always resolve to *C:\Users\{username}\AppData\Local\Temp.* To see a list of environment variables and their values, try typing set in a command window.

Example MSI Extraction

Let's look at how you could extract the MSI from the *FUSION Excel Connect Client 32bit.exe* application that has been used as an example throughout this chapter so far.

Double-click the exe installer to begin the installation. (See Figure 3-4)

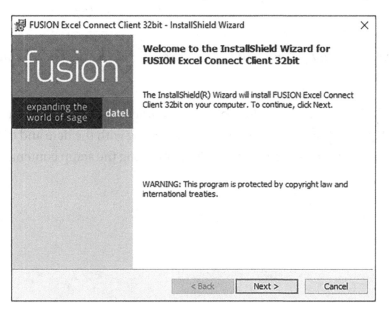

Figure 3-4. *Begin the MSI extraction process by manually running the setup.exe installation*

At this stage, this is far as you need to go, although on some Setups you may need to go to the next stage by clicking next. The main takeaway is that you do not click through to the stage where the installation would take place – you want to stop just before that process.

Leaving the Installation GUI on screen, type %temp% in the Run menu to view the contents of the temp directory. (See Figure 3-5)

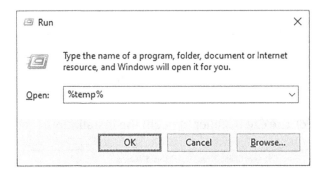

Figure 3-5. *Navigating to the Temp directory using the environment variable shortcut*

In the Temp directory, click the *Date Modified* title to view it in date order. Figure 3-6 shows only one entry coinciding with the date and time of extraction and this should be the folder containing the setup contents.

Figure 3-6. *Using detective skills to match the directory Date Modified time to the time the setup.exe was launched*

Double-click the matching folder, and there it is – the much sought-after prize. Copy the MSI to a different location and only then cancel the exe installation that was started. (See Figure 3-7)

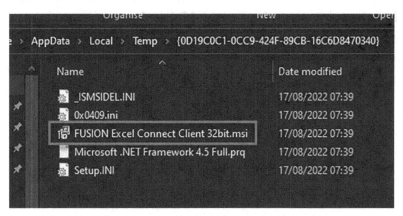

Figure 3-7. *Case closed: the MSI has been located and can be copied to another location before canceling the setup.exe installation*

Just like that, you have an MSI that can be deployed.

Setups can be a pain to deploy and sometimes no amount of effort will result in a deployable application. Having said that, take some solace that in over 15 years of application deployment I have only ever experienced this once.

Summary

This chapter has been a breeze compared to the previous ones. You have learned that the dreaded setup.exe application installer may not be as scary as it seems.

You learned that you could query the registry much as you would for MSIs for the same uninstall string information and were reminded of searching for online help or documentation that may assist in building the command line parameters required.

Failing all of that, you learned two simple MSI extraction techniques that, if successful, enable a far superior MSI deployment instead.

Next up, it's all about detection rules and their various types, and finally, you will see some PowerShell coding.

CHAPTER 4

Detection Rules

In Microsoft Intune, detection rules are used to determine the presence of a Win32 application. The detection rule will make sure that the application installation will only occur if it is not already installed and will also help to confirm a successful installation or not.

There are three types of detection rules built into Intune: MSI, file, and registry, and, for the most part, these will meet most of your needs. When they don't, you will need to resort to using custom PowerShell detection rules.

This chapter will start by going over some detection fundamentals before moving on to how detection scripts work and the logic behind them. You will then learn about the various types of detection rules, with examples of each type ready to use with your own deployments. Finally, you will learn about custom rules and branching.

Why Use PowerShell?

As well as the three native detection rules, a fourth, more advanced detection type is available to use, and that is a custom detection script – this allows you to script a detection rule for practically anything, limited only by your imagination, and you achieve this by using PowerShell.

Using PowerShell can be a time saver as once you have a detection script saved that you know works, it's a simple case of a small adjustment to two or three variables and uploading it to Intune – you can rest back on your chair, coffee in hand, knowing that the script has been tried-and-tested before and will do its job correctly.

© Owen Heaume 2022
O. Heaume, *Understanding Microsoft Intune*,
https://doi.org/10.1007/978-1-4842-8850-4_4

This book is all for repeatable and reliable deployments, and PowerShell detection rules are a part of that process.

Detection Fundamentals

Let's start by understanding what informs Microsoft Intune whether an application deployment has been successful or not.

The Microsoft Rules

Although the table in Figure 4-1 has been sourced from the Microsoft Configuration Manager documentation,[1] it is still relevant for Intune, and it shows how you can use the output of a script to determine if an application has been installed.

Script exit code	Data read from STDOUT	Data read from STDERR	Script result	Application detection state
0	Empty	Empty	Success	Not installed
0	Empty	Not empty	Failure	Unknown
0	Not empty	Empty	Success	Installed
0	Not empty	Not empty	Success	Installed
Non-zero value	Empty	Empty	Failure	Unknown
Non-zero value	Empty	Not empty	Failure	Unknown
Non-zero value	Not empty	Empty	Failure	Unknown
Non-zero value	Not empty	Not empty	Failure	Unknown

Figure 4-1. *Shows how the output of a script can signify a successful application install*

---

[1] https://docs.microsoft.com/en-us/previous-versions/system-center/system-center-2012-R2/gg682159(v=technet.10)#to-use-a-custom-script-to-determine-the-presence-of-a-deployment-type

Interpreting the Table

The part relevant to your scripted detection rule is the second column header: *Data read from STDOUT.*

STDOUT, or Standard Out, is a stream to which a program outputs its data. The way your detection script is going to use it is to output data to the screen by using a native PowerShell cmdlet.

Figure 4-2 (a cropped version of the table shown in Figure 4-1) shows it is the third row you are interested in: to signify a successful installation your script will need to write to the STDOUT data stream. In other words, if the data read from STDOUT is *not empty* (in other words, it has been written to), then the application detection state will be *installed.*

Script exit code	Data read from STDOUT	Data read from STDERR	Script result	Application detection state
0	Empty	Empty	Success	Not installed
0	Empty	Not empty	Failure	Unknown
0	Not empty	Empty	Success	Installed
0	Not empty	Not empty	Success	Installed

Figure 4-2. *If the data read from STDOUT is not empty then signify a successful app detection*

In Practice

To achieve this, the PowerShell cmdlet Write-Host is used in the detection script code, and you will have seen this cmdlet from Chapter 1, where you were encouraged to read the help files and try out the cmdlets for yourself.

The PowerShell help files for Write-Host state: *"Writes customized output to a host."* The host in this case is STDOUT. Sounds perfect.

Write-Host will display text to the screen, and if you need a refresher from Chapter 1, you use it like this:

```
Write-Host "Hello Reader, are you enjoying this book?"
```

To signify a successful deployment, you need to use Write-Host to send a message to the screen. But what message should you send? Well, anything! You could use: Write-Host "Success!" or: Write-Host "Installed" just as much as you could use: Write-Host "What a nice day! Are you enjoying it?" As long as you write *something* it will be interpreted as a successful detection by Intune.

Note   Even though Write-Host will output text to the screen, the end user will never see it when used in a detection script. It will, however, turn up in the IntuneManagementExtension.log found at C:\ProgramData\Microsoft\IntuneManagementExtension\Logs.

Where Do I Put the Detection Rules Anyway?

If you are coming from Microsoft Endpoint Configuration Manager (previously known as System Centre Configuration Manager or SCCM for short), then you may wonder if you can copy and paste your rules into a dialog box somewhere within the Intune portal. Currently, in Intune, this is not possible. You must create the detection rule in PowerShell, save it somewhere on your computers as a .ps1 file and then within the Intune portal, browse to the script location and select it to upload.

When you create a new application within the Intune management portal and select the type to be a *Windows app (Win32)*, detection rules are stage four of the creation process.

1. Select the drop-down list next to "Rules format" and choose "Use a custom detection script" from the available options.

2. Select the folder icon next to "Script file" which will then allow you to browse to and select your .ps1 detection rule that you will have previously created and saved.

Figure 4-3 highlights the correct areas you will need to modify to upload your detection scripts.

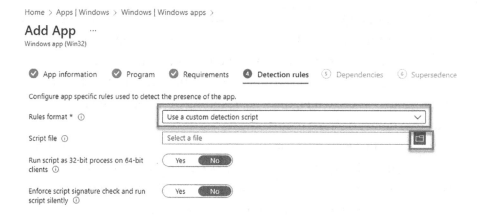

Figure 4-3. *Stage four of Win32 app creation. Uploading a custom detection script in the Intune portal*

Silently Continue

When crafting your own detection rules, you will often need to use the parameter -ErrorAction tacked onto the end of the relevant cmdlet being used.

This parameter allows the suppression of non terminating errors, and you should assign it the value of *SilentlyContinue.* (-ErrorAction ↵ SilentlyContinue)

A non terminating error is not as serious as a terminating error as it will not stop the script from running. This is in stark contrast to a terminating error which will immediately halt script execution.

Note   A terminating error cannot be silenced with the -ErrorAction parameter and if you want to handle them you should use try/catch blocks instead. That way if there is a terminating error, the code within the try block is halted and execution skips to the catch block where you can handle the error.

A non terminating error would otherwise prevent your detection script from doing its job properly. For example, if you were trying to validate a registry key on a system where the key did not exist, a non terminating error would be produced and written to STDERR (have another look at the table previously shown in Figure 4-1), resulting in script failure and the application detection state of unknown.

By adding the -ErrorAction SilentlyContinue parameter, the non terminating error is suppressed should it occur, allowing the script to continue to exit normally and generate the correct failure exit code.

It is probably easier to demonstrate this so let's try it out. In a PowerShell prompt, execute the following: Get-Item c:\thisdoesnotexist

Assuming there is not a folder or file named *thisdoesnotexist* at that location, a non terminating error will be written to STDERR, and a red error message will be presented on screen because, well, it doesn't exist. (See Figure 4-4)

Figure 4-4. The location doesn't exist and a sea of red is produced

Now try this: `Get-item c:\thisdoesnotexist -Erroraction`
`SilentlyContinue`

Nada. Nothing. Zilch. Diddly Squat. Error suppressed. (See Figure 4-5)

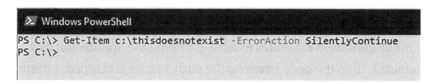

Figure 4-5. *This time the error is suppressed and nothing is displayed on the screen*

How Detection Scripts Work

The way a detection script works can be summarized in plain English as, *"Check if this condition is true, if it is, then it means the application has successfully installed and we should use Write-Host to let Intune know that."*

To summarize it even more succinctly, "If this, then that."

In PowerShell, you will use the IF statement to achieve the desired goal. The IF statement is followed by opening and closing brackets. Within the brackets is the condition that you wish to evaluate as being true. (Usually, this is the test condition that proves the application has been installed.) (See Listing 4-1.)

Listing 4-1. A simplified explanation of If...then

```
If <condition is true> then <Inform Intune installation was
successful>
```

In PowerShell, the then; part of the statement is represented by the curly braces { } and anything in between the curly braces is what should be executed in the event of the condition evaluating to true; like informing Intune the application install was successful. (See Listing 4-2.)

Listing 4-2. PowerShell If Statement construction – If this, then that

```
If (Condition is true) {
    <Inform Intune installation was successful>
}
```

If the IF condition evaluates to false, meaning the application was not detected, then the code between the curly braces is skipped, Intune is not informed of a successful installation by using `Write-Host` to write to STDOUT, and the script executes successfully with nothing written to either STDOUT or STDERR.

Consulting the first row in the table shown previously in Figure 4-1, you can see that having nothing written to STDOUT or STDERR, as well as a successful script execution, will signify to Intune that the application was not installed.

Detection Rule Types

Now that the fundamentals have been covered, it is time to look at the common detection rule types used in application deployment.

Note   As teaching PowerShell is beyond the scope of this book, I will not explain the minutiae of the inner workings of each detection rule, although if you have read the preceding chapters then you will have some basic understanding already. As with anything, you learn best by doing, and you should read the PowerShell help files on anything that you feel requires clarification and try the code out for yourself on a test computer.

File/Folder Presence

One of the simpler detection methods is to verify the existence of a file or folder.

To use the code examples shown in Listing 4-3, do the following:

- Set the $fileOrFolderName variable to the file or folder name to detect.

- Set the variable $path to the location of the file or folder to detect.

(You can add or leave trailing backslashes when setting the path variable as Join-Path sorts this out for you.) Listing 4-3 detects the presence of the text file: *All Servers.txt* stored in *C:\ohtemp*.

If the file is found, and therefore the condition has been evaluated to true, then Write-Host is invoked which outputs a message to the screen: "Detected!"

Listing 4-3. Detecting file existence

```
$fileOrFolderName = "All Servers.txt"
$path = "C:\ohtemp"

If (Test-Path (Join-Path -Path $path -ChildPath ↩
$fileOrFolderName)) {
    Write-Host "Detected!"
}
```

Testing for folder existence is achieved using the same method, specifying a folder name instead of a file name for the $fileOrFolderName variable.

Listing 4-4 demonstrates testing for the existence of a folder named, *Important Folder* located at *C:\ohtemp*.

Listing 4-4. Testing for folder existence

```
$fileOrFolderName = "Important Folder"
$path = "c:\ohtemp"

If (Test-Path (Join-Path -Path $path -ChildPath ↩
  $fileOrFolderName)) {
    Write-Host "Detected!"
}
```

Executable Presence

Executable detection is identical code to file or folder detection, the only difference being the variable named $fileOrFolderName has been renamed to $Executable for clarity; particularly important if other people may eventually use your scripts.

In Listing 4-5, the code detects the presence of the Java executable, *java.exe*, found in the path *C:\ProgramFiles(x86)\java\jre1.8.0_333\bin*

Note the use of the PowerShell environment variable: ${env:ProgramFiles(x86)} in the code.

Listing 4-5. Detecting the Java executable

```
$executable = "java.exe"
$path = "${env:ProgramFiles(x86)}\java\jre1.8.0_333\bin"

If (Test-Path (Join-Path -Path $path -ChildPath $executable)) ↩
{
    Write-Host "Detected!"
}
```

Executable Version

While the previous example of detecting the presence of a specific executable can be useful, often it is more helpful to detect the version number of the executable.

Continuing to use java.exe as the example executable, let us now make sure it is also the expected version number.

In this instance, the version number of the .exe is 80.3330.2 as shown by right-clicking the java.exe file and looking at the Details tab on the properties page. (See Figure 4-6)

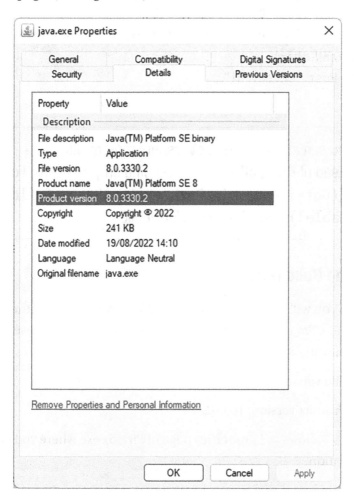

Figure 4-6. *Discovering the version number of the Java executable*

PowerShell can obtain this information using the cmdlet Get-Item, and Listing 4-6 demonstrates the detection rule for this process.

Listing 4-6. Detecting the product version of an executable file

```
$versionNumber = '8.0.3330.2'
$executable = "java.exe"
$path = "${env:ProgramFiles(x86)}\java\jre1.8.0_333\bin"

If ((Get-item (Join-Path -Path $path -ChildPath $executable) ↩
-ErrorAction SilentlyContinue).VersionInfo.ProductVersion ↩
-eq $VersionNumber) { ↩
    Write-Host "Detected!"
}
```

Note   You can also use the **FileVersion** property with `Get-Item` instead of **ProductVersion** depending on your needs. For example: `(Get-item (Join-Path -Path $Path -ChildPath $Executable)).VersionInfo.FileVersion`

Finding the Build Number

Sometimes you will want the complete build number to use in the detection rule. For example, the Firefox.exe properties page presents the following information:

- File version: 103.0.2.8255

- Product version: 103.0.2

Figure 4-7 shows the properties page of Firefox exe where you can view this information.

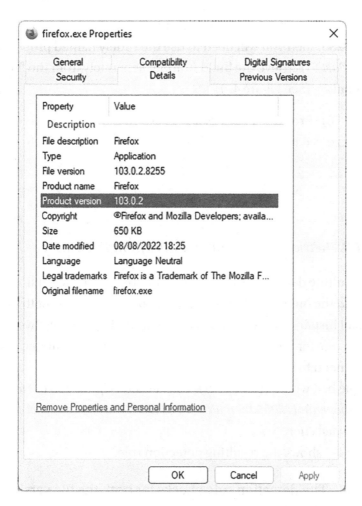

Figure 4-7. *The file version and product version of Firefox.exe*

If you use Get-Item to retrieve either the *file version* or *product version* of Firefox.exe, the only value returned is 103.0.2. (See Figure 4-8)

```
Administrator: Windows PowerShell
PS C:\> (Get-Item "C:\Program Files\Mozilla Firefox\firefox.exe").VersionInfo.fileversion
103.0.2
PS C:\>
```

Figure 4-8. *The value returned is 103.0.2 even though the file version is requested*

If your detection rule requires confirming the full file version number of *103.0.2.**8255***, then you will need to use the rudely named property, *FilePrivatePart* to retrieve the build number separately from the file version number. (See Figure 4-9)

```
(Get-Item "C:\Program Files\Mozilla ↩
Firefox\firefox.exe").VersionInfo.FilePrivatePart
```

Figure 4-9. *Retrieving the build number from Firefox.exe*

The resulting detection rule tests for both parts, the file version number *and* the build number, and expects both to be present to signify a successful installation. It does this by using -and to evaluate two conditions: one for the file version *and* one for the build number, and both conditions need to be true.

In English, it would read as, *"If the file version equals 103.0.2 **and** the build number equals 8255 then write to STDOUT to signify a successful application detection."*

Listing 4-7 shows the resulting detection rule.

Listing 4-7. The detection rule checks for both the file version and the build number

```
$versionNumber = '103.0.2'
$buildNumber = '8255'
$executable = "firefox.exe"
$path = "$Env:ProgramFiles\Mozilla Firefox"
```

```
If ((Get-item (Join-Path -Path $path -ChildPath $executable)
-ErrorAction ↵
SilentlyContinue).VersionInfo.FileVersion -eq $versionNumber -and
(Get-item ↵
(Join-Path -Path $path -ChildPath $executable) -ErrorAction ↵
SilentlyContinue).VersionInfo.FilePrivatePart -eq $buildNumber) {
    Write-Host "Detected!"
}
```

Registry Subkey

It is rare to only wish to detect the presence of a registry subkey. For accuracy, you would want to detect a specific value/data pair.

Should you need to though, the detection rule would resemble this. (By now I'm sure I don't need to tell you to adjust the variable $RegistrySubKey in the code to meet your needs.)

Figure 4-10 shows the Google Chrome registry subkey the detection rule in Listing 4-8 is testing for.

Figure 4-10. *The registry location of the Chrome subkey*

Listing 4-8. The detection rule for the Chrome registry subkey

```
$registrySubKey = "HKLM:\SOFTWARE\Google\Chrome"

If (Test-Path $registrySubKey) {
    Write-Host "Detected!"
}
```

Registry Value/Data Pair

Now, this is more like it. Often, when you are using the registry for detection rules, you will be trying to detect a specific value and its corresponding data to signify a successful deployment.

For this example, if you have deployed the application *Git for Windows* you may decide to use the registry as the detection rule.

You want to be certain that version 2.32.0.2 has been deployed and decide to detect its registry value *CurrentVersion* and its corresponding data. (See Figure 4-11)

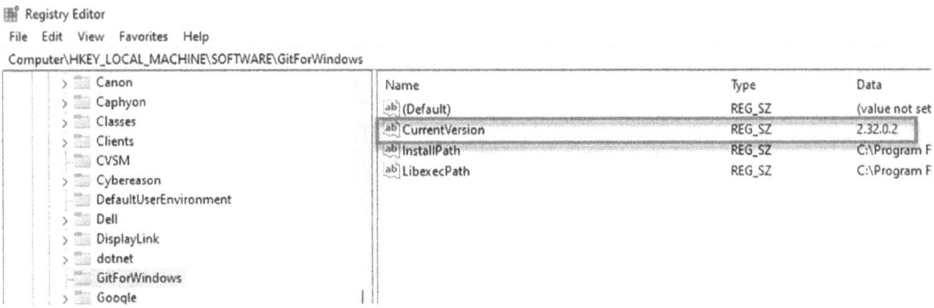

Figure 4-11. *Checking the registry for the value and data to use in the detection script*

The detection script to achieve this is shown in Listing 4-9.

Listing 4-9. Detection script for a registry value and data pair

```
$registryKey = 'HKLM:\SOFTWARE\GitForWindows'
$value = 'CurrentVersion'
$data = '2.32.0.2'

if ((Get-ItemProperty -Path $registryKey | Select-Object ↵
  $value -ExpandProperty $value -ErrorAction ↵
SilentlyContinue) -eq $data) {
    Write-Host "Detected!"
}
```

Why Don't You Just Silently Continue?

Perhaps an easier method to obtain the desired registry value/data would be to use the less complex detection rule shown in Listing 4-10.

Listing 4-10. An easier detection method to obtain registry value/ data maybe, but prone to error

```
$registryKey = 'HKLM:\SOFTWARE\GitForWindows'
$value = 'CurrentVersion'
$data = '2.32.0.2'

if ((Get-ItemPropertyValue -Path $RegistryKey -Name ↵
$Value -ErrorAction SilentlyContinue) -eq $data) {
    Write-Host "Detected!"
}
```

Sure, it will work, but remember earlier in this chapter when you were learning about -SilentlyContinue and the difference between non terminating and terminating errors? The cmdlet Get-ItemPropertyValue will produce a terminating error if the value it is looking for does not exist. (This may be the case in a failed deployment.)

If you recall, the -SilentlyContinue switch will not suppress terminating errors and data will be written to the STDERR stream, signifying an unknown outcome.

The trick here is to refactor the code and pipe the contents from Get-ItemProperty (which outputs terminating errors) to Select-Object (which outputs non terminating errors), and will therefore be our host for the -SilentlyContinue parameter.

EXERCISE

Try this for yourself: using the detection rule in Listing 4-10 (adjusting the variables to a valid registry value and data pair on your system), verify that the value is detected and "Detected!" is written to your screen.

Then edit the $value variable to something that does not exist and run the same code again. What do you get?

Even though the -silentlyContinue switch is used, it has not stopped the error because it is a terminating error that was produced.

Now try the same thing with the detection rule in Listing 4-9. This time, there is no error message as it has been successfully suppressed.

It is important to always test the code that you write and find out what will happen if what you are trying to detect is not there or contains invalid data. Make sure that it has the desired outcome.

While it may be quicker to use shortcuts and forgo testing your code, in the end, putting in the hard work and doing it properly will save you headaches in the future. And remember, code is reusable. Do it properly once and it's done forever, ready to be reused time and time again.

Custom Detection

There may come a time when you can't find anything to detect or don't care too much and wish to signify the deployment was successful regardless of any true verification.

What you are saying in situations like this is, *"I don't want to, or cannot validate that the application was successfully installed but I want to tell Intune that the installation was okay anyway."*

In edge cases like these (and there should be few instances where you need to do this), you can create a file, or registry subkey with associated value/data to detect as part of your deployment script and then validate its existence in the detection rules to signify a successful deployment, knowing it will always be a successful deployment.

An easier method still is to detect a default file or folder as these are already always present on Windows systems.

The following example detects the existence of cmd.exe, and you will have seen these very same detection rules used before in this chapter, just not for nefarious purposes like now! (See Listing 4-11.)

Listing 4-11. Detecting for cmd.exe – you know it will always be there

```
$executable = "cmd.exe"
$path = "$env:SystemRoot\system32"

If (Test-Path (Join-Path -Path $path -ChildPath $executable)) {
    Write-Host "Detected!"
}
```

Detecting for the presence of a default Windows system file as demonstrated by Listing 4-11 is the easiest method to achieve a lazy detection rule. Alternatively, you could opt for detecting a default folder guaranteed to be in place instead, and Listing 4-12 does just that, using the System32 folder for the detection rule.

Listing 4-12. Detecting the presence of the Windows\System32 installation directory

```
$fileOrFolderName = "System32"
$path = $env:windir

If (Test-Path (Join-Path -Path $path -ChildPath ↩
$fileOrFolderName)) {
     Write-Host "Detected!"
}
```

Custom File Detection

You may prefer to create a file to detect as part of the application deployment. Then, once the application has been installed the detection rule looks for the presence of the file just created, which, in turn, signifies a successful application detection.

One advantage of this method over detecting a default file or folder shown previously is that you can rename the created file on each updated deployment of the same application. For example, the first deployment of app1.exe creates an empty text file named App1-001.txt. If App1.exe is then updated and needs to redeploy, this time around the deployment creates and detects App1-002.txt.

As alluded to earlier, the text file is created in the same PowerShell script that deploys the application, and you should do this in the pre- or post-application install phase. It does not matter if you create the file before or after the application is installed because (and let's face the ugly truth here), if you are using this method of application detection then you are either unable to detect the application through conventional means, or, and I hope this is not the case, you just don't care.

When using this bad practice of detection, a good practice to follow is to create the custom files in a specific folder at a specific location, and out of reach of standard users.

You should write to the Windows directory, in a subdirectory named after the company you work for, followed by a directory called: Custom Detection. This fulfills two tasks: users are unable to delete its contents, (it is assumed that users log in with standard user permissions – if not you should ask yourself, "Why?"), and the directory then becomes the central storage area for any future projects you may end up working on where you need a repository for custom output or storage.

Here is an imaginary scenario to hammer home this concept.

Scenario: Yum-Yum Dog Foods Inc

Your manager approaches you with the following task: a new application, MyApp.exe, needs to be deployed to all staff.

You install the application on your test system and work out the installation command line.

You discover that once installed, there is no easy method of detecting the installation; having scoured the registry and file system you cannot find anything relevant to use as a detection rule.

You decide to use custom file detection and will create a file called: MyApp-001.log as part of the application deployment script and this can then be used in the detection rule you will write. You also add code to create the directory structure if it's not present; if the structure is already present it will just create the file to detect.

To use this code, replace the values for the variables: $companyName and $fileName where *Yum Yum Dog Foods Inc* is the name of the company you work for and *MyApp-001.log* is the name of the file to be created.

Listing 4-13 shows the PowerShell code used in the application deployment script to create the custom file.

Listing 4-13. PowerShell code for writing a custom file to be used by the detection script

```
$companyName = 'Yum Yum Dog Foods Inc'
$fileName = 'MyApp-001.log'

$detectionPath = Join-Path -Path "$env:SystemRoot" ↩
-ChildPath "$CompanyName\Custom Detection"

if (!(Test-Path $DetectionPath)) {
    New-Item -Path $DetectionPath -ItemType Directory | ↩
Out-Null
}

New-Item -Path $DetectionPath -Name $FileName -ItemType ↩
File -Force | Out-Null
```

Figure 4-12 shows the resulting file, MyApp-001.log, ready for detection. The file structure *Yum Yum Dog Foods Inc\Custom Detection* is created if it did not already exist, otherwise, just the file *MyApp-001.log* is created.

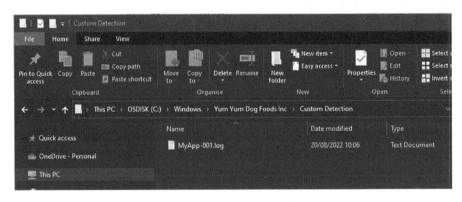

Figure 4-12. *Successful creation of the custom detection file*

You decide to use the code shown in Listing 4-14 to use as the detection rule.

Listing 4-14. The detection rule used for MyApp-001.log

```
$fileOrFolderName = "MyApp-001.log"
$path = "$env:SystemRoot\Yum Yum Dog Foods Inc\ ↵
Custom Detection"

If (Test-Path (Join-Path -Path $path -ChildPath ↵
$fileOrFolderName)) {
    Write-Host "Detected!"
}
```

Custom Registry Detection

You may prefer to write to the registry instead of the file system for your custom detection and, much like creating custom files, and for the same reasons, it's best to write to the registry in an organized structure; this keeps everything neat.

Continuing the previous scenario of working for Yum Yum Dog Foods Inc, here is where you could write in the registry:

```
HKEY_LOCAL_MACHINE\SOFTWARE\Yum Yum Dog Foods ↵
Inc\CustomDetection
```

Once again, the PowerShell code in Listing 4-15 will first check to see if this location exists in the registry already, and if not, create it before finally writing the value and data to be used for detection.

To use this code, replace the values for the variables, $companyName with the name of the company you work for, $applicationName with the name of the application you are deploying, and $value with the value you will detect in the detection rule: This can be anything, although, for simplicity, it's best to stick with sequential numbers starting from 0 or 1.

Listing 4-15. PowerShell code for writing a custom registry entry to be used by the detection script

```powershell
$companyName = 'Yum Yum Dog Foods Inc'
$name = 'MyApp'
$value = '1'

$registryPath = Join-Path -Path "HKLM:\SOFTWARE" ↵
-ChildPath "$companyName\Custom Detection"

if (!(Test-Path $registryPath)) {
    New-Item -Path $registryPath -Force | Out-Null
}

New-ItemProperty -Path $registryPath -Name $name ↵
-Value $value -PropertyType DWORD -Force | Out-Null
```

Figure 4-13 shows the resulting registry value and data pair ready for the custom detection rule.

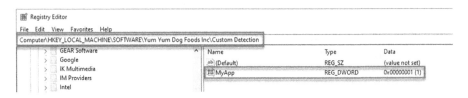

Figure 4-13. *Successful creation of the custom detection registry entry*

The detection rule that matches up with this is shown in Listing 4-16.

Listing 4-16. The rule to detect the custom registry data

```powershell
$registryKey = 'HKLM:\SOFTWARE\Yum Yum Dog Foods ↵
Inc\Custom Detection'
$value = 'MyApp'
$data = '1'
```

```
if ((Get-ItemProperty -Path $registryKey | Select- ↩
Object $value -ExpandProperty $value -ErrorAction ↩
SilentlyContinue) -eq $data) {
    Write-Host "Detected!"
}
```

Final Thoughts on Custom Detection

Don't use it! Joking aside, there may come a time when this is the only method available to you and it is good to have this knowledge in your toolbelt, just in case.

Remember though, creating items for custom rules to detect is not good practice and won't verify the deployed application is installed. They should only be used as a last resort. They do, however, get you out of a bind in times of need.

Branching

Sometimes you will want to detect either in one location or another depending on if a 32-bit or 64-bit installation has occurred.

A single deployment script can be configured to install either a 32-bit or 64-bit program depending on the target computer "bitness," and you may not know ahead of time if the detection rule needs to query inside of *Program Files (x86)* or *Program Files*.

Although not so common now, you may also wish to detect based on Microsoft Office bitness (e.g. a 32-bit Microsoft Office installation or a 64-bit Microsoft Office installation).

Solve these scenarios by using branching detection rules.

By Office Bitness

In this example detection rule, querying the installed Microsoft Office "bitness" will cause code execution to branch to the correct detection rule to use, based on if the query result is either 32-bit or 64-bit.

71

In English, the code reads something like this: "If the installed Office version is x86 (32-bit) then use this detection rule. If the Office version is x64 (64-bit) then use this other detection rule."

Edit each of the two if statements in the code sample shown in Listing 4-17 to detect whatever you need to signify a successful installation based on the installed Office "bitness."

Listing 4-17. A detection rule based on Microsoft Office "bitness"

```
$OfficePath = 'HKLM:\Software\Microsoft\Office'
$OfficeVersions = @('14.0','15.0','16.0')

foreach ($Version in $OfficeVersions) {
    try {
            Set-Location "$OfficePath\$Version\Outlook" ↵
 -ea stop -ev x
            $LocationSet = $true
            break
        } catch {
            $LocationSet = $false
        }
}

if ($locationSet) {
        switch (Get-ItemPropertyValue -Name "Bitness") {
        "x86" { if ( <# Detect something here - ↵
file existence, file version etc #> ) { Write-host ↵
"Installed!"}}
        "x64" { if ( <# Detect something here - ↵
 file existence, file version etc #> ) { Write-host ↵
 "Installed!"}}
        }
}
```

Note   Listing 4-17 will not run "as-is" as the two IF statements are missing conditions. Once you add the conditions to test for, the code will execute as expected. This is demonstrated in the next scenario.

Scenario – Detecting Mimecast

Mimecast is an application that has two installers: one 32-bit installer and one 64-bit installer. If the client computer has a 32-bit version of Microsoft Office installed, then the 32-bit version of Mimecast must be installed. Likewise, if the client computer has a 64-bit version of Microsoft Office installed then the 64-bit version of Mimecast needs to be installed.

In this scenario, the correct version of Mimecast has been installed and now a detection rule needs to be created that will detect successful installation by querying the correct installed location, either Program Files (x86) or Program Files.

The detection rule queries the "bitness" of the installed Microsoft Office version to determine which path (Program Files (x86) or Program Files) to check the file version of muspkg32.exe and ensure that it matches 7.6.0.11151, if it does, Write-Host is used to signify a successful installation. Listing 4-18 demonstrates this scenario.

Listing 4-18. Detecting Mimecast based on the "bitness" of Microsoft Office

```
$MimecastVersion = '7.6.0.11151'

$OfficePath = 'HKLM:\Software\Microsoft\Office'
$OfficeVersions = @('14.0','15.0','16.0')

foreach ($Version in $OfficeVersions) {
    try {
        Set-Location "$OfficePath\$Version\Outlook" ↩
-ea stop -ev x
```

```
        $LocationSet = $true
        break
    } catch {
        $LocationSet = $false
    }
}

if ($locationSet) {
    #Check for bitness then check correct file version
    switch (Get-ItemPropertyValue -Name "Bitness") {
        "x86" { if ((get-item ↩
        "${env:ProgramFiles(x86)}\Mimecast\Mimecast ↩
Outlook Add-In\musepkg32.exe" -ErrorAction ↩
SilentlyContinue).VersionInfo.fileversion -eq ↩
$MimecastVersion) { Write-host "Installed!"} }
        "x64" { if ((get-item ↩
        "$ENV:ProgramFiles\Mimecast\Mimecast ↩
Outlook Add-In\musepkg32.exe" -ErrorAction ↩
SilentlyContinue).VersionInfo.fileversion -eq ↩
$MimecastVersion) { Write-host "Installed!"}}
    }
}
```

Or What?

I wanted to demonstrate how you could use Office bitness in a detection rule for completeness; however, it's a bit of an overkill and complicated to read. Instead, using PowerShell's logical operator -or could be a better alternative and you may find this more suitable for future detection scripts that require branching of some kind.

It reads as this: *"If you have detected the correct executable version in Program Files (x86) OR if you have detected the correct executable version in Program Files, then inform Intune that installation was successfully detected."*

By using -or, it doesn't matter which path the executable file was found in that you are using for detecting the version number against – so long as it was found in *one* of the correct paths then it is a success.

Listing 4-19 demonstrates this using -or to detect if *musepkg32.exe* was installed in either Program Files (x86) *or* Program Files.

Listing 4-19. Using PowerShell -or operator in the Mimecast detection rule

```
$programFiles32 = (get-item ↩
"${env:ProgramFiles(x86)}\Mimecast\Mimecast ↩
 Outlook Add-In\musepkg32.exe" -ErrorAction ↩
SilentlyContinue).VersionInfo.FileVersion
$programFiles64 = (get-item ↩
"$ENV:ProgramFiles\Mimecast\Mimecast ↩
Outlook Add-In\musepkg32.exe" -ErrorAction ↩
SilentlyContinue).VersionInfo.FileVersion

if ($programFiles64 -eq '19.0.0.60' -or $programFiles32 ↩
-eq '10.0.19041.1') {
    Write-Host "Installed!"
}
```

This *and* This

In this last example, both versions of Java (32-bit and 64-bit) were deployed, and therefore for the deployment to be considered successful both versions of Java must be detected.

To do this, the detection queries the version number of Java.exe in both Program Files (x86) *and* Program Files to ensure they match the required value for the detection rule to signify success. Listing 4-20 demonstrates how this is achieved using the -and operator.

Listing 4-20. Detecting this and this to signify a successful detection

```
$VersionNumber = '8.0.3410.10'
$Executable = "java.exe"
$32BitPath = "${env:ProgramFiles(x86)}\Java\jre1.8.0_341\bin"
$64BitPath = "$env:ProgramFiles\Java\jre1.8.0_341\bin"

If ((Get-item (Join-Path -Path $32BitPath -ChildPath
$Executable) -ErrorAction ↩
SilentlyContinue).VersionInfo.ProductVersion -eq ↩
$VersionNumber -and (Get-item (Join-Path -Path ↩
$64BitPath -ChildPath $Executable) -ErrorAction ↩
  SilentlyContinue).VersionInfo.ProductVersion -eq ↩
$VersionNumber) {
    write-host "Installed!"
}
```

Tip   Both -or and -and are known as logical operators. To find out more information on these and other logical operators, try using the built-in help by typing the following in a PowerShell console: help About_Logical_Operators

---

Summary

Well, who knew there would be so much to learn about detection rules? This has been a long chapter and you have covered a lot of ground.

First, you learned about why you might use PowerShell for your detection rules, before moving on to some fundamentals. You learned how to deal with terminating and non terminating errors and how detection scripts work. There are a lot of different types of detection rules and by now you should be able to identify which detection rule will meet your needs. For those edge cases, you learned how to use custom detection rules which can get you out of a bind in times of need. Finally, you learned about detection rule branching.

In the next chapter, you will learn about more advanced application deployment scenarios involving additional file copy operations and where to place the files for deployment. The chapter also covers how to reference the files within the PowerShell deployment script.

CHAPTER 5

Location, Location, Location

There may be a requirement to copy files to specific locations pre- or post-application deployment. An application may require customization through a pre-configured INI (configuration) file for example, or some supporting documentation must be copied to the user's Documents folder, or perhaps additional corporate backgrounds must be deployed as part of a Microsoft Teams installation.

There can be many reasons why you may need to copy additional files along with the deployed application. In this chapter, you will learn where to place the files and how to reference them in the PowerShell deployment script depending on their location within the root folder structure.

Where Is This Script Running from Anyway?

If you always knew the file location your deployed script was in and the source files it referenced, it would be a fantastic thing indeed. If you knew the script was deployed to a client computer, executed from *C:\:MyKnownDirectory\MyScript.ps1* and the referenced files were in the same directory as the script then life would be magic.

When the script is downloaded to the endpoint, it will be downloaded to *C:\Windows\IMECache* – the folder containing the actual script and source files will be in a subfolder of *IMECache* that is a random GUID.

© Owen Heaume 2022
O. Heaume, *Understanding Microsoft Intune*,
https://doi.org/10.1007/978-1-4842-8850-4_5

Alas, when deploying scripts using Endpoint Manager you have no idea of the random GUID subfolder containing the script and any accompanying source files essential to the deployment.

You need to discover where the script is running from, only then will you be able to reference the files for copy commands to work successfully. After all, copy commands work by copying from a known source location to a destination. How can this be achieved without knowing the source?

How We Used to Do Things

In the good old days, you would write a batch file and use %~dp0 to reference the current location.

The %~dp0 variable, when referenced within a Windows batch file, will expand to the drive letter and path of the batch file. This meant you would never need to know where the batch file was running from.

The task now is to find the same solution using PowerShell. In the early days of PowerShell, the solutions provided were convoluted with syntax that was hard to remember. Have a look at the following PowerShell syntax:

```
$MyInvocation.MyCommand.Path | Split-Path -Parent
```

Ugly, right? Will it work? Sure, and there is certainly a place for the $MyInvocation automatic variable[1] and it is capable of so much more; however, for your deployment needs there must surely be a more elegant solution.

---

[1] https://docs.microsoft.com/en-us/powershell/module/microsoft. powershell.core/about/about_automatic_variables?view=powershell-7.2&v iewFallbackFrom=powershell-7.1

A Better Way

Since PowerShell version 3, there is an easier method of determining where a PowerShell script is being executed from.

The automatic variable $PSScriptRoot contains the full path of the executing script's parent directory. It doesn't get much easier than that.

You will learn how to use this automatic variable to reference files later in this chapter, but first, there needs to be an agreed method on how the files will be structured, and that's next.

File Placement

At a minimum, you will always have two files somewhere in a directory that will make up the deployment package you will learn how to create later in the book: the PowerShell .ps1 script that will take care of the deployment and the application that will be deployed. Beyond that, there may be additional files required as part of the deployment, and deciding where to place these files inside the directory is a matter of personal preference. The only difference will be how you reference the files within a PowerShell deployment script.

Flat-File Placement

In a flat-file placement, there is no file structure. All files, regardless of type, are placed in a single directory and Figure 5-1 demonstrates this.

Figure 5-1. *Everything in a single directory*

Advantages of Using a Flat-File Structure

Using this method for storing all files in a single directory can be a quick option when you are only deploying an application or have only a single file type for each file that needs deploying. (Having a single file type negates the need for filters in subsequent PowerShell code, and you will see an example of using a filter later in the book using the Copy-Item cmdlet.)

Structured File Placement

In a structured approach, you should leave the deployment script in the root directory. For every file type to be deployed, including the application itself, a subdirectory is created to contain the appropriate files.

A structured file placement would resemble something like that shown in Figure 5-2.

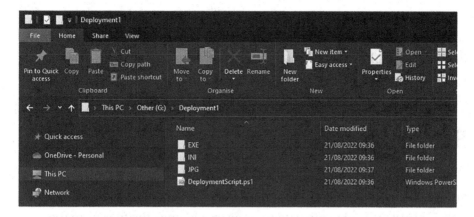

Figure 5-2. *A structured file placement*

In Figure 5-2, the root directory is named Deployment1 and contains the following:

– The PowerShell DeploymentScript.ps1 in the root

– Subdirectory named EXE to contain the application Setup.exe

– Subdirectory named INI to contain the INI files

– Subdirectory named JPG for the image files

Advantages of Using a Structured Approach

Not only is a structured approach more visually appealing (imagine if there were 50 or more other files to deploy), but there are also advantages to using this method.

For example, if you are copying all files in the JPG subdirectory to a destination, you can reference the source location as \JPG*.* to copy everything contained within it. This simplifies the PowerShell code as you do not need to filter out the other file types when using the Copy-Item cmdlet. (Discussed later in the book.)

Whether all files are placed in a root directory or multiple subdirectories is an entirely personal preference. Just ensure the PowerShell deployment script or template you are using is always in the root location for ease, the rest doesn't matter.

Referencing Files

Now that some thought has been given to where to place the files, and you know how to obtain the location that the script is being executed from, ($PSScriptRoot), it is time to learn how to reference the files from the PowerShell script.

First Things First

Whether you are using a deployment template or a custom PowerShell script, somewhere near the beginning of the script you should set the current working directory to the root path of where the script is being executed from.

You do this by using the PowerShell cmdlet Set-Location.

```
Set-Location $PSScriptRoot
```

PowerShell's Set-Location is akin to the DOS CD (change directory) command. Having set the location to the current working directory of the script, it is now very easy to reference other files that are in the root directory.

Referencing Files in a Flat Structure

As the current script location has already been set (Set-Location $PSScriptRoot) all that is required to reference files is to precede the filename with .\ (period backslash).

.\ means the path is relative to the current directory.

For example, to reference an MSI called App1.msi you would use the following syntax in the PowerShell deployment script: .\App1.msi

Referencing a text file is the same: .\MyTextFile.txt

I should point out that you can also use the automatic variable itself to reference the files should you prefer to: $PSScriptRoot\App1.msi or $PSScriptRoot\MyTxtFile.txt and, arguably, it may make for better code legibility.

Referencing Files in Subdirectories

To reference files that are more structured and organized is as simple. If you have changed to the working directory of the script execution path in your deployment script (Set-Location $PSScriptRoot) then you can reference the files using the following syntax: ".\MySubdirectory\My Text File.txt".

Alternatively, you could achieve the same thing using the automatic variable $PSScriptRoot using the following syntax: "$PSScriptRoot\MySubdirectory\My Text File.txt".

Note the use of quotes in the above examples. While not necessary in all cases, if you have a space anywhere in the path then quotes are required. As a habit, you should always use quotes even if the file path does not contain spaces.

Tip   Using $PSScriptRoot when referencing files instead of .\ negates the requirement of adding Set-Location $PSScriptRoot in your PowerShell deployment script as it already contains the full path to where the script is being executed from.

Here is a brief example for additional clarification: let's say there is an image file called Wallpaper.jpg and it's in a subdirectory of the root called Images. (See Figure 5-3)

Figure 5-3. *The Wallpaper.jpg file you need to reference*

If you have added the code Set-Location $PSScriptRoot at the start of your PowerShell deployment script, then the file would be referenced like this:

.\Images\Wallpaper.jpg If you have not added the Set-Location code or you just want to anyway, you could reference the file using $PSScriptRoot because it already contains the full path of the script execution location. In this case, you can reference the file using the following syntax: $PSScriptRoot\Images\Wallpaper.jpg.

To Me, To You, and Back Again

There may be a requirement where you must change the working directory from the script execution root path to an entirely new path by a different PowerShell provider.

You can do this by referencing the full path directly in the relevant PowerShell cmdlet.

Take the following scenario as an example:

The deployment script contains `Set-Location $PSScriptRoot` right at the very start of the script. The current working directory has now been set and the rest of the PowerShell code uses this to its advantage: various procedures are performed and files are referenced by beginning the path with `.\` – for example, `.\SubDirectory1\SubDirectory2\image1.jpg`.

Let's say the script must now perform a lot of registry manipulation in the *HKLM:\Software\MyCompany* and *HKLM:\Software\MyCompany\ Attributes* keys.

You could do this by specifying the full registry path in the cmdlets being used like so: `New-ItemProperty -Path "HKLM:\Software\MyCompany"` ↵
`-Name "EmpNo01" -Value 001 | Out-Null`

Listing 5-1 shows some example code of how this might look, and Figure 5-4 shows the resulting code execution.

Listing 5-1. Writing to the registry - a different location to $PSScriptRoot

```
Clear-Host

set-location $PSScriptRoot

Write-host "The current location is: $(Get-Location)" ↵
-ForegroundColor Cyan

Write-host "Making changes to the registry..." ↵
-ForegroundColor DarkCyan

New-ItemProperty -Path "HKLM:\Software\MyCompany" -Name ↵
"EmpNo01" -Value 001 | Out-Null
New-ItemProperty -Path "HKLM:\Software\MyCompany" -Name ↵
"EmpNo02" -Value 002 | Out-Null
New-ItemProperty -Path "HKLM:\Software\MyCompany\ ↵
Attributes" -Name "New01" -Value 001 | Out-Null
```

```
New-ItemProperty -Path "HKLM:\Software\MyCompany\ ↵
Attributes" -Name "New02" -Value 002 | Out-Null
```

```
Write-host "Registry changes have been made." ↵
-ForegroundColor DarkCyan
```

```
Write-host "The current location is: $(Get-Location)" ↵
-ForegroundColor Cyan
```

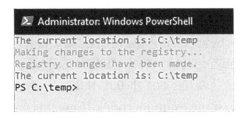

Figure 5-4. *Shows the outcome of Listing 5-1*

Code Breakdown

1. Line 1: The screen is cleared using `Clear-Host`.

2. Line 3: The current working directory is set to the path that the script is being executed from.

3. Line 5: `Write-Host` is used to display the working path which is *C:\temp*.

4. Lines 9–12: Various changes are made to the registry using the `New-ItemProperty` cmdlet. Note the `-path` parameter contains the full location of the registry key being manipulated.

5. Line 16: The registry changes have been made and `Write-Host` is used to display that the working location has not changed. It is still in *C:\temp*.

Now, there is nothing wrong with this method, but if you are changing location back and forth a lot in your script then there is another method that you should be aware of.

Push/Pop-Location

There are two PowerShell cmdlets that you can use to effortlessly change to a different location and back again: Push-Location and Pop-Location.

Push-Location

Push-Location is like Set-Location in that it will change to a new working directory. (Also like the DOS CD (change directory) command.)

The main and crucial difference is that it will remember where it came from. It "pushes" the current location to a location stack and if specified, will then change the current location to the location specified in the path. If the current location is C:\Temp and you wish to change location to C:\Windows the syntax is as follows: Push-Location C:\Windows

When you are ready to return to the original location (C:\Temp), you use the cmdlet: Pop-Location.

Pop-Location

The Pop-Location cmdlet changes the current location to the location most recently pushed onto the stack by using the Push-Location cmdlet. You do not need to add any parameters to Pop-Location to return from whence you came.

Let's Try This Again

Changing to a new location using Push-Location now enables you to reference paths more easily using .\ (period backslash). You can push to locations all over the place knowing that with a simple pop you can easily revert to the location you just came from.

Listing 5-2 demonstrates how the code in Listing 5-1 might look if Push-Location and Pop-Location were used instead of full paths to the registry keys, and Figure 5-5 shows the outcome of the code execution.

Listing 5-2. Using Push-Location and Pop-Location to change to a new working directory and back again

```
Clear-Host

set-location $PSScriptRoot

Write-host "The current location is: $(Get-Location)" ↩
 -ForegroundColor Cyan

Write-host "Changing location to the relevant registry ↩
key in HKLM." -ForegroundColor Cyan
push-location "HKLM:\software\MyCompany"

Write-host "Push-Location. Current location is: ↩
$(Get-Location)" -ForegroundColor Yellow

Write-host "Making changes to the registry..." ↩
-ForegroundColor DarkCyan

New-ItemProperty -Path . -Name "EmpNo01" -Value 001 | Out-Null
New-ItemProperty -Path . -Name "EmpNo02" -Value 002 | Out-Null
New-ItemProperty -Path ".\Attributes" -Name "New01" ↩
 -Value 001 | Out-Null
New-ItemProperty -Path ".\Attributes" -Name "New02" ↩
-Value 002 | Out-Null
```

```
Write-host "Registry changes have been made." ↵
 -ForegroundColor DarkCyan

Pop-Location

Write-host "Pop-Location. The current location is: ↵
 $(Get-Location)" -ForegroundColor Cyan
```

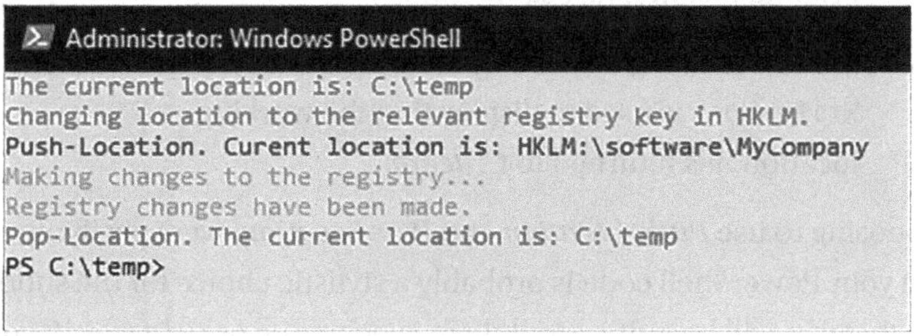

Figure 5-5. *Shows the outcome of Listing 5-2*

Code Breakdown

1. Line 1: The screen is cleared using `Clear-Host`.

2. Line 3: The current working directory is set to the path that the script is being executed from.

3. Line 5: `Write-Host` is used to display the working path which is *C:\temp.*

4. Line 8: `Push-Location` is used to change the working directory to a registry location, *HKLM:\ software\MyCompany.*

5. Line 10: `Write-Host` is used to display the working path which is now *HKLM:\software\MyCompany.*

6. Lines 14–17: Various changes are made to the registry using the New-ItemProperty cmdlet. Note the -path parameter now contains current path abbreviations (. and .\) to reference the required registry locations of the registry keys being manipulated.

7. Line 21: Pop-Location is used to return to the original location just came from.

8. Line 23: The registry changes have been made and Write-Host is used to display that the working location has returned to *C:\temp*.

Choosing to use *Push-Location* and *Pop-Location* over specifying a full path in your PowerShell code is probably a stylistic choice for the short scripts that you will be writing and there is no wrong or right way. If you find that you are hopping around all over the place in your code, then it might make more sense to use these two cmdlets.

I chose to include it in this book as it is something that I always use and have used in the sample Deployment Template script that you will learn about later in the book – and as my intention is for you to fully understand all aspects of the script, it made sense then, to explain it here.

Summary

A short but tough chapter this one. You learned how to find out where the deployed PowerShell script is being executed from and then the two different ways you could place your files needed for a deployment.

It was explained how to reference those files and then how to reference new locations that are not held by the $PSScriptRoot automatic variable.

Finally, you learned an alternative method of navigation between locations using the Push-Location and Pop-Location cmdlets.

In the next chapter, you will learn how to invoke the installation of the application itself.

CHAPTER 6

Installing the Application

Installing the application is going to be the primary purpose of the deployment script and in Chapter 2 you learned that msiexec.exe was the tool to use. However, you cannot just enter msiexec.exe and the command line straight into your PowerShell script and expect it to work, it needs to be called from a PowerShell cmdlet first.

In this chapter, you will learn how to install either an MSI or setup.exe using PowerShell and the associated common cmdlet parameters.

Start Your Engines Please

Well, the subtitle is a bit misleading here because you're not starting an "engine" per se, more a process, using the native PowerShell cmdlet: Start-Process.

You will be pleased to know that if you need to install either an MSI or a setup.exe, the same cmdlet is used.

The Start-Process cmdlet will do exactly as its name suggests, and reading the help file for it shows that it is very flexible in what it can do; not just launching programs (such as msiexec.exe) directly, but also, by specifying a *nonexecutable* file the cmdlet will start the program associated with the file.

© Owen Heaume 2022
O. Heaume, *Understanding Microsoft Intune*,
https://doi.org/10.1007/978-1-4842-8850-4_6

Parameters

The cmdlet Start-Process has a lot of parameters; however, you tend to use only four. Let's look at these in a bit more depth to see how and why you would use them.

-FilePath

This parameter must be supplied with a path to an executable, and depending on which one you are going to install (MSI or EXE) the -filepath parameter will be different.

MSIEXEC

This is where you will specify the path to msiexec.exe and you should remember to use the PowerShell built-in environment variables wherever you can.

Only include the msiexec.exe installer program here, you do not specify the actual MSI file that you are going to install.

```
Start-Process -Filepath "$ENV:SystemRoot\System32\msiexec.exe"
```

EXE

If you are deploying a setup.exe, then you must specify the path and name of the executable.

As explained in Chapter 5, your deployment script should contain the code Set-Location $PSScriptRoot to set the current working directory to that which the script is being executed from.

You are then able to reference the setup.exe using the shorthand of .\ (remember, . (a period by itself) means the current directory).

```
Start-Process -Filepath ".\Setup.exe"
```

Alternatively, you can reference the working directory path using the automatic variable $PSScriptRoot which holds the path that the script is being executed from:

```
Start-Process -Filepath "$PSScriptRoot\Setup.exe"
```

Whether you use .\ or $PSScriptRoot to reference the root path, remember to include any subdirectories in it if you are storing the setup.exe elsewhere:

```
Start-Process -Filepath "$PSScriptRoot\EXE\7z1900-x64.exe"
```

Note   Although I have demonstrated including the path to msiexec. exe or the setup.exe in the -Path parameter, you could also use the -WorkingDirectory parameter for this instead, and then only specify the EXE name in the path parameter. I tend not to use this parameter, but for clarity, you may prefer to in your scripts. The syntax for msiexec.exe would then be as follows: `Start-Process -FilePath "msiexec" -WorkingDirectory "$ENV:SystemRoot\System32"` and for a setup.exe you would use `Start-Process -FilePath "Setup. exe" -WorkingDirectory "$PSScriptRoot"`.

-ArgumentList

This parameter is where you will add the program arguments.

Minimum Information

For a setup.exe, as a minimum, you will want to add the argument to signify a silent installation should occur.

For an MSI you will need to signify that an installation should take place by using the /i parameter (or /x should you wish to uninstall), followed by the path to, and name of the MSI installation file and then the silent install switch.

You may have additional parameters or properties to set, depending on what you are trying to achieve, and they may be added here too, after the MSI name.

Finally, encapsulate the whole thing in quotes:

```
-ArgumentList "/I .\myMSI.msi /qn /norestart"
```

-NoNewWindow

This parameter starts the new process in the current console window. By default, PowerShell opens a new window, and you don't want that.

-Wait

This parameter suppresses the command prompt and retains the window until the process has finished. In other words, *"Don't do anything else until the application has finished installing."*

Don't miss this parameter out or your script may go a bit screwy if you are adding post-deployment tasks that are dependent on the MSI or setup. exe installation to complete first.

Dealing with Spaces

What if you have spaces in the MSI file name? For example, if the MSI was named: Mimecast for Outlook 7.6.0.26320 (32 bit).msi (True story!)

Of course, you could always rename the file and remove the spaces but luckily, the solution is rather simple: enclose the *path* and *MSI* name in *double quotes* in the -ArgumentList parameter like so:

```
-ArgumentList ""$PSScriptRoot\Mimecast for Outlook 7.6.0.26320
(32 bit).msi""
```

Putting It All Together

Now that you have learned about the individual parameters required for a successful installation to occur using Start-Process, it's time to put it all together with some examples.

Example 1 – Simple MSI

Listing 6-1 demonstrates a silent installation of the 64-bit version of 7-Zip using the MSI installer.

Listing 6-1. A silent installation of an MSI

```
Start-Process -Filepath "$ENV:SystemRoot\System32\↩
msiexec.exe" -ArgumentList "/i $PSScriptRoot\7z1900-x64.msi /qn
/norestart"
```

Example 2 – MSI with Properties

Listing 6-2 demonstrates a silent install of Java using the MSI installer as well as setting several MSI properties.

Listing 6-2. A silent installation of an MSI including the setting of additional properties

```
Start-Process -FilePath "$ENV:SystemRoot\System32\↩
msiexec.exe" -ArgumentList"/i $PSScriptRoot\↩
jre1.8.0_191.msi /qn JAVAUPDATE=0 AUTOUPDATECHECK=0 ↩
IEXPLORER=1 REBOOT=Suppress" -NoNewWindow -Wait
```

Example 3 – Setup.Exe

Listing 6-3 demonstrates silently installing the 64-bit version of 7-Zip using the executable installer and passing the argument for a silent installation.

Listing 6-3. A silent installation of a setup.exe

```
start-process -FilePath ".\7z1900-x64.exe" -ArgumentList ↩
"/S" -NoNewWindow -Wait
```

Summary

Compared to the five previous chapters, this was a short one. You learned how to use PowerShell to deploy either an MSI or a setup.exe, the parameters you should use, and why you use them. You also learned what to do if the command line included spaces, and finally were shown three examples of how to call your installation using the Start-Process cmdlet.

In the next chapter, you will learn about deploying a PowerShell script or template and the subtle nuances of each script type.

CHAPTER 7

Deploying the Script

Once you have a PowerShell script or deployment template ready to go, you will need to understand the command line required to deploy it in Intune.

This is the moment you have been building up to, pacing up and down like an expectant father. Like Doctor Frankenstein's monster, it is time to give this thing life: it is time to deploy it using the Intune Management Portal, Win32 App creation.

In this chapter, you will learn how to construct the correct install commands that are input into the Intune Portal when creating a new Win32 application deployment.

Sys What Now?

The Intune Management Extension is a 32-bit application that executes PowerShell scripts or processes Win32 applications.

In most cases, whenever a 32-bit application attempts to access *%windir%\System32* or *%windir%\regedit.exe*, the access is redirected to an architecture-specific path, for example, *%windir%\SysWOW64*, where 32-bit versions of the file being accessed are used instead.

The management extension executes in the 32-bit context resulting in the deployed PowerShell script also executing in the 32-bit version of PowerShell running from SysWOW64.

This may not have the outcome you desire and could cause deployment failure, as some cmdlets require running in a 64-bit context. Other unexpected results may occur too: the cmdlet Get-Process, for

O. Heaume, *Understanding Microsoft Intune*,
https://doi.org/10.1007/978-1-4842-8850-4_7

example, will only get 64-bit processes in 64-bit PowerShell and 32-bit processes in 32-bit PowerShell which may or may not be what you are expecting. In general, you will always want your PowerShell script to run in the 64-bit version of PowerShell.exe

To avoid this situation, there is another folder, called Sysnative, and it can be used as a replacement for System32 in the path name.

Sysnative as a special alias is used to indicate that the file system should not redirect the access. When you specify C:\Windows\Sysnative in your code or application, it is diverted to C:\Windows\System32 instead.

Solution

To ensure the PowerShell script executes using the 64-bit version of PowerShell, a small modification must be made to the "Install Command" and/or "Uninstall Command" fields in the Intune portal. You must reference the full path of the 64-bit version of PowerShell.exe using Sysnative in place of System32.

32-Bit PowerShell

If you deliberately wish to use the 32-bit version of PowerShell, then you can reference the executable from:

```
C:\Windows\syswow64\WindowsPowerShell\v1.0\powershell.exe
```

Tip In the Intune portal "Install command" field, you can reference powershell.exe directly, omitting the full path. This is because the Intune Management Extension will be running in a 32-bit process and will therefore call PowerShell.exe from a 32-bit process by default.

Note the 32-bit version is in the SysWOW64 directory. You can prove this PowerShell version is 32-bit by typing `C:\Windows\syswow64\WindowsPowerShell\v1.0\powershell.exe` in the Run dialog box to launch the PowerShell console, and then typing `[System.Environment]::Is64BitProcess`. The output will be `False`, in answer to the question, "Is this a 64-bit process?" (See Figure 7-1.)

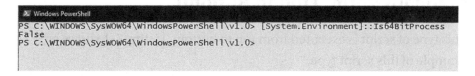

Figure 7-1. *Running 32-bit PowerShell from SysWOW64 directory*

64-Bit PowerShell

When creating the command line to use from within the Intune portal, you must reference 64-bit PowerShell.exe using the full path and substitute System32 with Sysnative:

`"C:\Windows\System32\WindowsPowerShell\v1.0\PowerShell.exe"`

   is replaced by

`"C:\Windows\Sysnative\WindowsPowerShell\v1.0\PowerShell.exe"`

Calling Your Script

Once you have a PowerShell deployment script, you will need to ask yourself the following questions about it:

- Is it just a script that executes sequentially from top to bottom?

- Does it have an entry point?

- Does it have an entry point with parameters?

101

- Is it a function?

- Does the function accept parameters?

The script type determines which command line is used within the Windows Win32 App creation in the Intune Portal.

Standard Script (Top to Bottom)

This type of script is executed from top to bottom. Listing 7-1 shows an example of this script type.

Listing 7-1. A script that executes from top to bottom

```
# This is an example of a standard script.
# It is executed sequentially from top to bottom.
[int]$ValueA = 10
[int]$ValueB = 20
[Int]$Total = $ValueA + $ValueB

Write-Output "I have just done some incredible things ↩
with this script!"
Write-Output "Including adding up two values! ↩
The answer is: $Total"
```

Install Command

Listing 7-2 shows the install command to use for a standard script.

Listing 7-2. The install command for a standard script. (Top to Bottom)

```
"C:\Windows\Sysnative\WindowsPowerShell\v1.0\↩
PowerShell.exe" -noprofile -executionpolicy ↩
bypass -file .\myScript.ps1
```

Script with Entry Point

Like the Standard Script (Top to Bottom), the same command line is used.

This type of script allows for more flexibility as the entire code is encapsulated as a function. The very last line of code that is then outside of that function will call the function itself which may or may not accept parameters too.

Script with Entry Point (No Parameters)

Listing 7-3 shows an example of a script with an entry point. The script is executed top to bottom and the entry point within the script itself calls the function to do the clever stuff.

Listing 7-3. A script containing an entry point and not using any parameters

```
Function Invoke-ApplicationInstall {
    # This function does some clever deployment stuff here
}

# The next line (line 6) is the script entry point:
Invoke-ApplicationInstall
```

Install Command

Listing 7-4 shows the full command line to use with this type of script.

Listing 7-4. The command line for a script with an entry point. (No Parameters used)

```
"C:\Windows\Sysnative\WindowsPowerShell\v1.0\PowerShell.exe" ↩
-noprofile -executionpolicy bypass -file .\myScript.ps1
```

Script with Entry Point (With Parameters)

Deploying a script with an entry point which calls a function with parameters is the same as without parameters. The exception is the entry point calling the function includes the desired parameters. Listing 7-5 demonstrates this.

Listing 7-5. A script with an entry point containing parameters

```
Function Invoke-ApplicationInstall {
      [CmdletBinding()]
      Param (
      [Parameter(Mandatory=$true)]
      [ValidateSet("x64","x86")]
      [String]$Architecture,
      [Parameter(Mandatory=$true)]
      [ValidateNotNullorEmpty()]
      [String]$Text
      )

 # This function does some clever deployment here...

}

# Script entry point with parameters of -Architecture ↵
and -Text:
Invoke-ApplicationInstall -Architecture x64 ↵
-Text "Some important text"
```

Install Command

Listing 7-6 shows the full command line to use with this type of script.

Listing 7-6. The command line for a script with an entry point using parameters

```
"C:\Windows\Sysnative\WindowsPowerShell\v1.0\PowerShell.exe" ↵
-noprofile -executionpolicy bypass -file .\myScript.ps1
```

Function

To directly reference a function in a script, a slightly different method must be used. To create the installation command line for scripts that include a specific function you wish to execute, you will use something called dot sourcing.

Normally, a script runs in the script scope meaning you do not have direct access to the functions, variables, etc., that it contains.

Dot sourcing allows you to run the script in the current scope, and all the commands in the script are available as if you had typed them at the command prompt.

To use dot sourcing, place a . (period) and a space before the script path.

For example:

```
. C:\myScripts\myScript.ps1
```

or

```
. .\myScript.ps1
```

You can read all about dot sourcing by typing in help about_scripts in a PowerShell console.

Note   You will notice that the command line for functions includes an & sign (ampersand). This is known as a call operator, and you can use it to execute scripts using their filenames. You can find out more about operators by reading the built-in help: help about_operators.

Function (No Parameters)

Let us say you have written a super-duper function called, *Do-Something*, and it is contained in a script named, *Function.ps1*. Listing 7-7 demonstrates what the function may look like.

Listing 7-7. A function containing no parameters. The script is saved as "Function.ps1"

```
function Do-Something {

 [CmdletBinding()]

 param ()

    Process {
        write-output "I'm doing something really cool"
    }
}
```

Install Command

In this example, the script has been saved as "Function.ps1" and the name of the function to run is named "*Do-Something.*"

Listing 7-8 demonstrates the installation command line to use.

Listing 7-8. A sample function that does not contain parameters. The function has been saved as "Function.ps1"

```
"C:\Windows\Sysnative\WindowsPowerShell\v1.0\PowerShell.exe" ↩
-noprofile -executionpolicy bypass -command "& ↩
{ . .\function.ps1; Do-Something}"
```

Function Accepting Parameters

Like deploying a function without parameters, the command line used is the same, except you add the required parameters and respective values.

For this example, let us pretend you have a script named, *myScript. ps1* and within this script, there is a function named, *Show-Text*. The function accepts a single parameter named, $textToDisplay. Based on the supplied parameter, the function then goes on to do something spectacularly amazing when executed.

Listing 7-9 demonstrates the function for this.

Listing 7-9. A function that accepts parameters

```
function Show-Text {
    [CmdletBinding()]

        param (
        [parameter (Mandatory=$true)]
        [string]$textToDisplay
        )

        Process {
            write-output "I'm doing something really cool ↵
using the supplied parameter of: $textToDisplay"
        }
}
```

Install Command

The goal here is to

- Call the script named, myScript.ps1

  - Specifically execute within the script the function named *Show-Text*.

- Supply the function parameter *-textToDisplay* with the value of "Important Text!"

Listing 7-10 demonstrates the command line to achieve this.

Listing 7-10. The command line used to call a function using parameters

```
"C:\Windows\Sysnative\WindowsPowerShell\v1.0\PowerShell.exe" ↵
-noprofile -executionpolicy bypass -command "& ↵
{ . .\myScript.ps1; Show-Text -textToDisplay "Important ↵
Text!" }"
```

Example: Deploying a Script Containing Two Functions

There may come a time when you have a single script containing multiple related functions. For example, your script may include one function for installation and another function for uninstallation.

As Intune allows you to specify two command lines, one for installation and one for uninstallation, then this is a good reason to use two public functions in a single script.

> **Note**   This example does not walk you through the complete
> creation of the application, as you will learn this later in the book.
> Rather, it demonstrates the deployment of a complex script, that
> is *only* a script (no additional files are deployed to the endpoint),
> with the script containing two functions; each of which can be used
> independently within the same Intune application creation.

Remote Server Administration Tools

This example script deploys the RSAT[1] (Remote Server Administration
Tools) capabilities for Windows 10 and contains the code to uninstall it
too if required. It is achieved using two functions in a single script saved as
"ManageRSAT.ps1".

The two functions are

- Install-RSATCapabilities

- Uninstall-RSATCapabilities

Listing 7-11 displays the full contents of the script.

Listing 7-11. ManageRsat.ps1

```
function Install-RSATCapabilities {

    [CmdletBinding()]

    param()

    BEGIN {
```

---

[1]https://docs.microsoft.com/en-us/windows-server/remote/remote-server-administration-tools

```powershell
        $Components = @('Rsat.Dns.Tools~~~~0.0.1.0',↵
'Rsat.GroupPolicy.Management.Tools~~~~0.0.1.0',↵
'Rsat.ActiveDirectory.DS-LDS.Tools~~~~0.0.1.0',
                       'Rsat.DHCP.Tools~~~~0.0.1.0',↵
'Rsat.FileServices.Tools~~~~0.0.1.0','Rsat.IPAM.Client.
Tools~~~~0.0.1.0', ↵
                       'Rsat.VolumeActivation.
Tools~~~~0.0.1.0','Rsat.↵
CertificateServices.Tools~~~~0.0.1.0','Rsat.BitLocker.↵
Recovery.Tools~~~~0.0.1.0')

        $val = Get-ItemProperty -Path ↵
"HKLM:\SOFTWARE\Policies\Microsoft\Windows\WindowsUpdate↵
\AU" -Name "UseWUServer" | select -ExpandProperty ↵
UseWUServer -ErrorAction SilentlyContinue
        Set-ItemProperty -Path ↵
"HKLM:\SOFTWARE\Policies\Microsoft\Windows\WindowsUpdate↵
\AU" -Name "UseWUServer" -Value 0 -ErrorAction ↵
SilentlyContinue
        Restart-Service wuauserv -ErrorAction SilentlyContinue
    }

    PROCESS {
        foreach ($Component in $Components) {
            $InstallState = (Get-WindowsCapability ↵
-Name $Component -Online -ErrorAction SilentlyContinue)↵
.state
            if ($InstallState -eq "NotPresent") {
                Write-Verbose "Adding: $Component..."
                Add-WindowsCapability -Online -Name ↵
$Component -ErrorAction SilentlyContinue
            } else {
```

```
            write-verbose "$Component already present."
        }
    }
}

END {
    Set-ItemProperty -Path "HKLM:\SOFTWARE\Policies\
Microsoft\Windows\WindowsUpdate↵
\AU" -Name "UseWUServer" -Value $val -ErrorAction ↵
SilentlyContinue
    Restart-Service wuauserv -ErrorAction SilentlyContinue
    }
}

function Uninstall-RSATCapabilities {

    [CmdletBinding()]

    param()

    BEGIN {

        $Components = @('Rsat.Dns.Tools~~~~0.0.1.0',↵
'Rsat.GroupPolicy.Management.Tools~~~~0.0.1.0',↵
'Rsat.ActiveDirectory.DS-LDS.Tools~~~~0.0.1.0', ↵
                        'Rsat.DHCP.Tools~~~~0.0.1.0',↵
'Rsat.FileServices.Tools~~~~0.0.1.0','Rsat.IPAM.Client.↵
Tools~~~~0.0.1.0',↵
                        'Rsat.VolumeActivation.Tools~~~~0.0.1.0',↵
'Rsat.CertificateServices.Tools~~~~0.0.1.0','Rsat.↵
BitLocker.Recovery.Tools~~~~0.0.1.0')

        $val = Get-ItemProperty -Path "HKLM:\SOFTWARE\Policies\
Microsoft\Windows\WindowsUpdate↵
\AU" -Name "UseWUServer" | select -ExpandProperty ↵
```

```
UseWUServer -ErrorAction SilentlyContinue
        Set-ItemProperty -Path ↵
"HKLM:\SOFTWARE\Policies\Microsoft\Windows\WindowsUpdate↵
\AU" -Name "UseWUServer" -Value 0 -ErrorAction ↵
SilentlyContinue
        Restart-Service wuauserv -ErrorAction SilentlyContinue
    }

    PROCESS {
        foreach ($Component in $Components) {
            $InstallState = (Get-WindowsCapability ↵
-Name $Component -Online -ErrorAction SilentlyContinue)↵
.state
            if ($InstallState -eq "Installed") {
                Write-Verbose "Uninstalling: $Component..."
                Remove-WindowsCapability -Online ↵
-Name $Component -ErrorAction SilentlyContinue
            } else {
                write-verbose "Cannot uninstall $Component ↵
as it is not present on this system."
            }
        }
    }

    END {
        Set-ItemProperty -Path "HKLM:\SOFTWARE\Policies\
Microsoft\Windows\WindowsUpdate↵
\AU" -Name "UseWUServer" -Value $val -ErrorAction ↵
SilentlyContinue
        Restart-Service wuauserv -ErrorAction SilentlyContinue
    }
}
```

When creating the Win32 application in the Intune portal, at stage two of the application creation wizard "Program," you should enter the install command line for a function accepting parameters (as shown previously in this chapter in Listing 7-10).

The full installation command line is shown in Listing 7-12.

Listing 7-12. Calling the Install-RSATCapabilities function from the ManageRSAT.ps1 script

```
"C:\Windows\Sysnative\WindowsPowerShell\v1.0\powershell.exe" ↩
-noprofile -executionpolicy Bypass -command "& ↩
{ . .\ManageRSAT.ps1; Install-RSATCapabilities }"
```

The uninstall command line is similar, except this time you call the uninstall function Uninstall-RSATCapabilities, as shown in Listing 7-13.

Listing 7-13. Calling the Uninstall-RSATCapabilities function from the ManageRSAT.ps1 script

```
"C:\Windows\Sysnative\WindowsPowerShell\v1.0\powershell.exe" ↩
-noprofile -executionpolicy Bypass -command "& ↩
{ . .\ManageRSAT.ps1; uninstall-RSATCapabilities }"
```

Figure 7-2 shows the completed install and uninstall command line at stage two of the Intune Win32 application creation wizard.

113

Home > Apps | Windows > Windows | Windows apps >

Add App ⋯
Windows app (Win32)

✓ App information   ❷ Program   ③ Requirements   ④ Detection rules   ⑤ Dependencies   ⑥ Supersedence (pre

Specify the commands to install and uninstall this app:

Install command * ⓘ   "C:\Windows\Sysnative\WindowsPowerShell\v1.0\powershell.exe" -noprofile -e... ✓

Uninstall command * ⓘ   "C:\Windows\Sysnative\WindowsPowerShell\v1.0\powershell.exe" -noprofile -e... ✓

Install behavior ⓘ   (System   User)

Device restart behavior ⓘ   App install may force a device restart   ⌄

Specify return codes to indicate post-installation behavior:

Figure 7-2. *The install command and uninstall command have been completed*

Figure 7-3 shows a portion of the Win32 application summary screen in the Intune portal where you can view the complete install and uninstall commands.

Program

Install command   "C:\Windows\Sysnative\WindowsPowerShell\v1.0\powershell.exe" -noprofile -
executionpolicy Bypass -command "& { . .\ManageRSAT.ps1; Install-
RSATCapabilites }"

Uninstall command   "C:\Windows\Sysnative\WindowsPowerShell\v1.0\powershell.exe" -noprofile -
executionpolicy Bypass -command "& { . .\ManageRSAT.ps1; uninstall-
RSATCapabilites }"

[Previous]   [**Create**]

Figure 7-3. *The full commands used can be seen in the application summary*

This deployment also uses a PowerShell custom detection rule and demonstrates the power and flexibility you can only get when using a PowerShell detection rule. It is shown in Listing 7-14.

Listing 7-14. The PowerShell script used for the RSAT deployment custom detection rule

```
$Components = @('Rsat.Dns.Tools~~~~0.0.1.0',↩
'Rsat.GroupPolicy.Management.Tools~~~~0.0.1.0',↩
'Rsat.ActiveDirectory.DS-LDS.Tools~~~~0.0.1.0', ↩
'Rsat.DHCP.Tools~~~~0.0.1.0','Rsat.FileServices.↩
Tools~~~~0.0.1.0','Rsat.IPAM.Client.Tools~~~~0.0.1.0',↩
'Rsat.VolumeActivation.Tools~~~~0.0.1.0','Rsat.↩
CertificateServices.Tools~~~~0.0.1.0','Rsat.BitLocker.↩
Recovery.Tools~~~~0.0.1.0')
 foreach ($Component in $Components) {
    $InstallState = (Get-WindowsCapability -Name ↩
$Component -Online -ErrorAction SilentlyContinue).state
        if ($InstallState -eq "Installed") {
            $Result = $true
        } else {
            $result = $false
            break
        }
}

if ($result) {
    write-host "Installed!"
}
```

Summary

In this chapter, you learned about the virtual folder Sysnative, and understood why it was important to use it when creating the script install or uninstall commands.

You then learned that not all scripts are the same; some have entry points, some have functions, and some are either of those types with parameters. You also learned how to build the correct install command line depending on which of those script types it was.

Finally, you saw an example of deploying the RSAT (Remote Server Administration Tools) that contained both an install and uninstall function, and what the install command lines would look like.

The next chapter looks at a fully functional deployment template that can be used as-is or modified for your own needs.

CHAPTER 8

Deployment Template

Using a deployment template can greatly speed up your application deployments and they offer many advantages over writing a separate script each time you wish to deploy an application. Once you have written a template and ironed out all the bugs then you end up with something that offers advanced functionality and is repeatable and reliable.

With a template, the hard work has already been done and you just have to "fill in the blanks."

In this chapter, you will learn all about the basic deployment template I wrote, and how to use it.

What It Does

This template can achieve the following:

- It can install based on Microsoft Office "bitness."

- It can install based on operating system architecture.

- It can process pre-installation tasks.

- It can process post-installation tasks.

- The installation includes a log file.

© Owen Heaume 2022
O. Heaume, *Understanding Microsoft Intune*,
https://doi.org/10.1007/978-1-4842-8850-4_8

The Template

To make sense of this chapter, it is best to open Listing 8-1 in the PowerShell ISE and follow along. If you do not want to (or cannot), it has been reproduced here in the book for convenience although the line wrapping and lack of coloration will make it less readable.

Listing 8-1. The full PowerShell template

```
Function Invoke-PreInstallation {
    # Anything you do here will occur **before** the ↵
    installation...
    # Perhaps copy some files, register some DLLs or ↵
    anything else you can think of!
}

function Invoke-PostInstallation {
    # Anything you do here will occur **after** the ↵
    installation...
    # Perhaps copy some files, register some DLLs or ↵
    anything else you can think of!
}

Function Invoke-ApplicationInstall {

    # Installs applications depending on office bitness or ↵
    os bitness
    # To install using Office bitness, use the switch ↵
    -InstallBasedOnOfficeBitness
    # To install based on OS architecture ↵
    (32-bit or 64-bit) do not use the switch

    [CmdletBinding()]
```

```powershell
    Param (
        [Switch]
        $InstallBasedOnOfficeBitness
    )

    Begin {
        $WorkingDir = Get-Location
        $LoggedInUser = (Get-CimInstance -ClassName ↩
CIM_ComputerSystem).username | Split-Path -Leaf
        $OSArchitecture = (Get-CimInstance -ClassName ↩
CIM_OperatingSystem).OSArchitecture $OfficePaths = ↩
        @('HKLM:\Software\Microsoft\Office','HKLM:\↩
Software\WOW6432Node\Microsoft\Office')
        $OfficeVersions = @('14.0', '15.0', '16.0')

        Push-Location

        foreach ($Path in $OfficePaths) {
            foreach ($Version in $OfficeVersions) {
                try {
                    Set-Location "$Path\$Version\Outlook" ↩
-ea stop -ev x
                    $Bitness = Get-ItemPropertyValue ↩
-Name "Bitness" -ea stop -ev x
                    switch ($bitness) {
                        'x86' {$Is32Bit = $True}
                        'x64' {$Is32Bit = $false}
                    }
                    break
                } catch {
                    $Is32Bit = 'Unknown'
                }
            }
```

```
            if ($Is32Bit -eq $true -or $Is32Bit -eq $false) {break}
        }

        $Obj = [pscustomobject]@{
            CurrentUser    = $LoggedInUser
            OfficeIs32Bit = $Is32Bit
            OSis64Bit      = if ($OSArchitecture -eq ↵
'64-Bit') {$True} else {$false}
        }

        Pop-Location
    }

    Process {
        # --- PRE-INSTALL SECTION ---

        Invoke-PreInstallation

        # --- END PRE-INSTALL ---

        if ($InstallBasedOnOfficeBitness) {
            # Install the application depending on if ↵
Microsoft Office is 64bit or 32bit or not installed
            # $True = Office is 32bit - Use this part to ↵
install 32bit applications
            # False = Office is 64bit - Use this part to ↵
install 64bit applications
            # Unknown = Office may not be installed.

            switch ($Obj.OfficeIs32Bit) {
                $true {"Install a 32-bit application here"}
                $false {"Install a 64-bit application here"}
                'Unknown' {"Office not detected - ↵
do what you want here"}
            }
        }
```

```
        else {
            # Installs a 64bt or 32bit application ↵
depending on the OS Architecture.
            # $True = The OS Architecture is 64-bit ↵
- Use this part to install the 64-bit application.
            # default = The OS is 32-Bit ↵
- Use this part to install the 32-bit application.

            switch ($obj.OSIs64Bit) {
                $True {start-process -FilePath ↵
"$ENV:SystemRoot\System32\msiexec.exe" ↵
-ArgumentList "/i ""$workingDir\Your64-BitMSI"" ↵
/qn" -NoNewWindow -Wait}
                default {start-process -FilePath ↵
"$ENV:SystemRoot\System32\msiexec.exe" ↵
-ArgumentList "/i ""$workingDir\Your32BitMSI"" ↵
/qn" -NoNewWindow -Wait}
            }
        }

        # --- POST-INSTALL SECTION ---

        Invoke-PostInstallation

        # --- END POST-INSTALL SECTION

    }

    End {
        # Write what the discovered object values are to a log.
        # This may help in troubleshooting.
        # Feel free to expand this section to include ↵
anything else that you want logged.
```

```
        "Logged In User: $($Obj.CurrentUser)" ↵
| out-file -FilePath ".\Invoke-ApplicationInstall.log" ↵
-ErrorAction SilentlyContinue
        "Office Version is 32Bit: $($Obj.OfficeIs32Bit)" ↵
| out-file -FilePath ".\Invoke-ApplicationInstall.log" ↵
-Append -ErrorAction SilentlyContinue
        "Operating System is 64Bit: $($Obj.OSis64Bit)" ↵
| out-file -FilePath ".\Invoke-ApplicationInstall.log" ↵
-Append -ErrorAction SilentlyContinue
    }
}

#Script entry point
Invoke-ApplicationInstall
```

The Template – Explained

When you examine the PowerShell code for this template there will be two mindsets: those with little to no PowerShell experience will be thinking it looks complex, and those with some PowerShell experience will be thinking, "*Is that it?*" And really, the mindset should be of the latter because the reality is, that this is a simple template.

The template consists of three functions and one switch. Let us start with an overview of each one to better understand how it works.

Function 1: Invoke-PreInstallation

Any code you place in this section will be executed before (or *pre*) the application is deployed. Any additional code you add needs to be between the curly braces. ({ and })

Examples of code I have placed in these sections are usually copying files to a specific location on an endpoint, but you could do anything that PowerShell allows. Just understand that it will execute *before* Function 3.

> **Note**   You should understand that PowerShell is a script and not a compiled language. Scripts are executed from top to bottom, line-by-line, and therefore if a function has not yet been defined first, then it cannot be called later in the script. Function 1 and Function 2 are called by Function 3, and so must be defined in the script *before* Function 3 so that they are ready to be used.

Function 2: Invoke-PostInstallation

Any code you place in this section will be executed after (or *post*) the application is deployed. Any additional code you add needs to be between the curly braces. ({ and })

Examples of code I have placed in these sections are usually along the lines of registering DLLs, registry modifications to customize the application that was just installed, or copying/replacing application INI files.

Once again, you are only limited by the constraints of PowerShell. Code placed in this section will occur *after* Function 3.

Function 3: Invoke-ApplicationInstall

This function is the meat-and-potatoes of the template. Here you can customize the install based on Microsoft Office "bitness," or operating system architecture.

Begin Block

Ignoring the switch for the moment, the code in the Begin { } block starts by setting the current location to the location that the script is being executed from and then populates various variables such as the logged-in user, the operating system architecture, and registry paths where one might expect to find Microsoft Office information if it were installed. The information stored in these variables will be used later.

The current location is pushed to the location stack via the Push-Location cmdlet and then a nested foreach loop is used to iterate through the Microsoft Office registry locations where an attempt is made to set the location using the Set-Location cmdlet, to the "Outlook" registry subkey. If the location can be set, then the "bitness" value is obtained, and the variable $Is32Bit is set to either $true or $false, depending on the value.

Figure 8-1 shows one of the registry locations being tested.

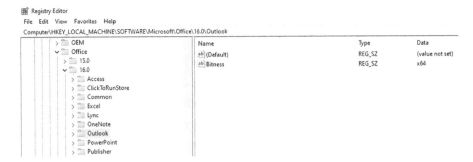

Figure 8-1. *This Office location exists, and you can see that the Office bitness is x64. $Is32Bit is set to $False*

Next, a custom PowerShell object is created to store the information obtained thus far and it will be accessed later. You do not need to use a custom object here; standard variables would work just as well, it is just my preferred method. You can read all about custom objects in the Microsoft documentation.[1]

Finally, because the working location was potentially changed to a registry location, the working location is set back to the script execution location using the cmdlet Pop-Location.

---

[1] https://docs.microsoft.com/en-us/powershell/scripting/learn/deep-dives/everything-about-pscustomobject?view=powershell-7.2

Process Block

The process block is where the application installation will take place.

Before that can happen, Function 1 is called: Invoke-PreInstallation. This will ensure that any pre-install tasks are carried out before the program installation occurs.

If the application is to be deployed based on Office "bitness," then that occurs next. If the application must be installed only if Microsoft Office has been detected and is 32-bit, then your application install command line must be entered in between the curly braces of the $true statement. (Replacing the text, "*Install a 32-bit application here*")

If the application must be installed only if the detected Office version is 64-bit, then the application install command line must be entered between the curly braces of the $false statement.

If you wish to do something if Office was not detected, then add code between the curly braces of the Unknown statement.

Figure 8-2 is a snippet taken from the full template code in Listing 8-1 that shows the locations where you would enter the application installation command, which could be an MSI or a Setup.exe, for this scenario.

```
71
72          switch ($Obj.OfficeIs32Bit) {
73              $true {"Install a 32-bit application here"}
74              $false {"Install a 64-bit application here"}
75              'Unknown' {"Office not detected - do what you want here"}
76          }
77      }
```

Figure 8-2. *Lines 73, 74, and 75 show the locations where you should add the application install commands for Office "bitness." Although you can add command lines to all three places, you only need to add them to the ones you wish to action*

Installing the application based on detected Operating System architecture is tackled next.

If the switch to install based on Office "bitness" was *not* used, then the application will default to installing based on if the operating system architecture is a 32-bit or 64-bit installation of Microsoft Windows.

If you wish to only install the application if the detected architecture is 64-bit, then the application installation command line must be entered between the curly braces of the $true statement. Likewise, enter the installation command line between the curly braces of the default statement to only install the application if the detected architecture is 32-bit.

Figure 8-3 is a snippet taken from the full template code in Listing 8-1 that shows the locations where you would enter the application installation command for this scenario.

```
82
83        switch ($obj.OSIs64Bit) {
84            $True {start-process -FilePath "$ENV:SystemRoot\System3
85            default {start-process -FilePath "$ENV:SystemRoot\Syste
86        }
```

Figure 8-3. *Lines 84 and 85 show the locations where you should add the application install commands for installing based on operating system architecture. Although you can add command lines to both places, you only need to add them to the ones you wish to action*

Once the application has been installed, a call to Function 2 is made: Invoke-PostInstallation. This will execute any desired code after the application installation has taken place.

End Block

The end block is the last code section to execute in Function 2 and it adds basic logging. It will write a log file containing the current logged-in username, the detected Microsoft Office "bitness" and finally whether the installed operating system is 32-bit or 64-bit.

The log file is named, *Invoke-ApplicationInstall.log*, and can be found in the *\Windows\temp* directory.

The Switch

The template contains a single switch, $InstallBasedOnOfficeBitness. This is defined near the top of Function 3 and it is optional to use when calling the script. If it is used, then the application will only install based on the detected Office "bitness." If the switch is not used, then the application will install based on the detected operating system architecture.

Figure 8-4 shows the location of the switch definition in the full template code from Listing 8-1.

```
17      [CmdletBinding()]
18
19 ⊟    Param (
20          [Switch]
21          $InstallBasedOnOfficeBitness
22      )
23
```

Figure 8-4. *Line 21 is where the switch has been defined*

You can read all about switches from the built-in PowerShell help, and by now you should be very familiar with the help about_ commands:

```
help about_switch
```

The Template Command Line

This template uses a script entry point, and the final line of code in the template calls the main function (Function 3) to set the whole process running:

```
Invoke-ApplicationInstall
```

The installation command line to use within the Intune portal when creating an application using this template is shown in Listing 8-2.

Listing 8-2. The template installation command for Intune

```
"C:\Windows\Sysnative\WindowsPowerShell\v1.0\PowerShell.exe" ↵
-noprofile -executionpolicy bypass -file ↵
.\Invoke-ApplicationInstall.ps1
```

This template has been written as a demonstration of a simple working example. You are free to use this as-is, modify it to suit your requirements, or use it as the basis of a template you write.

It was written to demonstrate basic template structures and concepts and has room for improvement in many areas. For example, you can add more extensive logging, encapsulate the various parameters as functions (such as deploying based on Office "bitness"), which can then be called directly from the installation command line instead of using a script entry point, or perhaps all your endpoints are 64-bit, and you can remove some of the redundant system architecture code.

The world is your oyster, and you should now feel confident to perform some of these modification tasks yourself or even write a template of your own from scratch.

Summary

In this chapter, you learned why you might use a template and examined the code of a ready-to-use example template. You learned how each part of the example template was constructed, and how to use it for your deployments.

In the next chapter, you will learn about preparing the application so that it may be imported into Intune for deployment.

CHAPTER 9

Application Preparation

You cannot directly upload an MSI or Setup.exe along with the associated PowerShell deployment script to Intune. The files must first be packaged together and uploaded as a single *intunewin* file.

In this chapter, you will learn how to download the intunewin creation tool and how to package your deployment that is acceptable to Intune.

Intunewin

The Microsoft Win32 Content Prep Tool is an application that converts installation files into the intunewin format required by Intune. It is a free download made available on Github.com by Microsoft and is straightforward to use.

Download the Content Prep Tool

The first step is to download the content prep tool. To do so, visit *https://github.com/Microsoft/Microsoft-Win32-Content-Prep-Tool* using your browser of choice. Figure 9-1 demonstrates where to download the ZIP file.

Figure 9-1. *Download the Microsoft Win32 Content Prep Tool from Github.com*

Before you extract the contents of the downloaded ZIP file it needs to be unblocked. Do this by right-clicking the ZIP file and choosing properties. On the properties page tick (check) the unblock box and click the OK button.

Figure 9-2 shows where you need to perform this action.

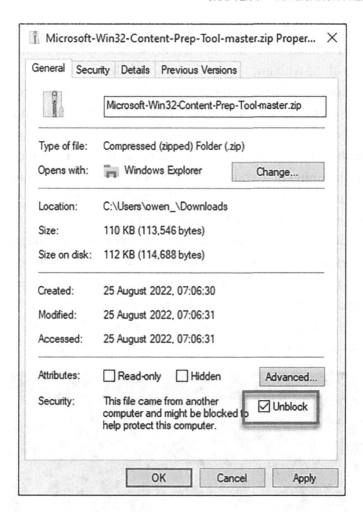

Figure 9-2. *Unblocking the downloaded ZIP file*

The ZIP file contents can now be extracted.

Prepare to Prep

Before running the content prep tool, it is useful to create an input and output directory.

The input directory is used to store the source files to be deployed and this will contain the PowerShell deployment script and associated application along with any required additional files.

The output directory will hold the resulting .intunewin file created by the content prep tool, and that can be imported into the Intune portal to create the final application.

Create both the input and output folder in a root directory named something meaningful to yourself, such as App Repository or Intune Apps.

The result will leave you with the following base structure:

C:\Intune Apps\input and *C:\Intune Apps\output.*

Keep yourself organized: within the input folder, create a single subdirectory for each application that will be converted into an intunewin file. You do not need to do the same for the output folder as the conversion process creates a single file named after the application.

Figure 9-3 shows what the input subfolder will look like if the Notepad++ application was going to be prepared for conversion.

Figure 9-3. *The contents of the input folder*

By creating subfolders for each application, you will end up with a central repository for all your application source files and this could come in handy in the future.

If having a source file repository is important to you, you may wish to take this a step further by creating an additional subdirectory named after the application version number. Something like this: C:\Intune Apps\ Input\Notepad++\8.4.4

Adding the Content

At this point, you can add the PowerShell deployment script, application, and source files to the input directory in the relevant application subdirectory.

You can choose to add all files to the root of the application subdirectory or as I prefer, to have more of a structured approach. This was discussed earlier in Chapter 5.

Whichever approach you take, leave the deployment script in the root application folder.

As an example, let us say you were tasked with deploying the Notepad++ application and additionally had to place a (fictitious) copy of the Notepad++ pdf help manual in the user's documents folder. Figure 9-4 shows how the application subfolder may look if the unstructured approach is used and Figure 9-5 shows how the application folder looks with a structured approach.

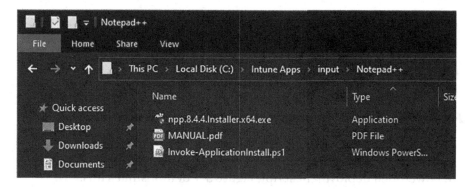

Figure 9-4. *An unstructured approach to file placement*

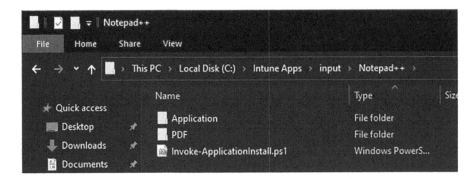

Figure 9-5. *A structured approach to file placement*

Converting the Source Files

Now that the source files are in place, it is time to convert them into a single intunewin file so that it can be uploaded into the Intune portal.

Begin by launching the IntuneWinAppUtil.exe that you downloaded. (It does not install and executes directly so you can place this file where it is most convenient for you to run.)

You are prompted for the source folder location, so type that in. Figure 9-6 continues with the Notepad++ example used so far in this chapter.

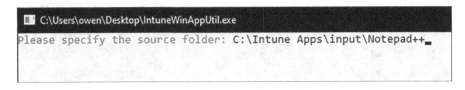

Figure 9-6. *Specify the source path to the application*

It then requests the setup file name. Here you must enter the name of the PowerShell deployment script. Figure 9-7 demonstrates this.

```
C:\Users\owen\Desktop\IntuneWinAppUtil.exe
Please specify the source folder: C:\Intune Apps\input\Notepad++
Please specify the setup file: Invoke-ApplicationInstall.ps1_
```

Figure 9-7. *Entering the name of the PowerShell deployment script*

You are then asked for the path to the output folder. Figure 9-8 demonstrates this.

```
C:\Users\owen\Desktop\IntuneWinAppUtil.exe
Please specify the source folder: C:\Intune Apps\input\Notepad++
Please specify the setup file: Invoke-ApplicationInstall.ps1
Please specify the output folder: C:\Intune Apps\output
```

Figure 9-8. *Adding the path to the output folder*

Finally, you are asked if you would like to specify a catalog folder. Make sure you type *n* for no. (Catalog files are used for Windows 10 S mode.) Figure 9-9 demonstrates this.

```
C:\Users\owen\Desktop\IntuneWinAppUtil.exe
Please specify the source folder: C:\Intune Apps\input\Notepad++
Please specify the setup file: Invoke-ApplicationInstall.ps1
Please specify the output folder: C:\Intune Apps\output
Do you want to specify catalog folder (Y/N)?n_
```

Figure 9-9. *A catalog folder is not required*

The IntuneWinAppUtil will then start the conversion. This only takes a few seconds and when it has finished the application will close.

If you check in the output directory there will be the resulting intunewin file that can be uploaded to Intune. Figure 9-10 shows the intunewin file in the output directory. Note the file is named after the PowerShell deployment script.

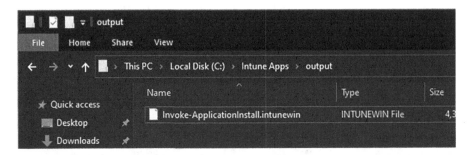

Figure 9-10. *The source files were successfully converted into an intunewin file*

Note   The application size is capped at 8GB. If your application is over this size, then you will need to look at an alternative method of deploying it as this solution will not work.

What's in a Name?

Well not much, as it turns out. When using the content prep tool and it asks "Please specify the setup file," if you recall in the Notepad++ example, the name of the PowerShell Deployment script (Invoke-ApplicationInstall.ps1) was input.

As it happens, you could also enter the "setup.exe" name or the MSI name instead should you wish to. It makes no difference because the final install command line that will be used in the Intune portal will be completely different and not a direct call to the executable \ MSI.

What it will do, however, is use this input as the *name* for the intunewin file it creates, and that is useful for your application repository.

However, there is something worth knowing and it only works for MSI files.

Although the deployment will use a PowerShell deployment script, you can enter the MSI name instead of the script name. (For example, *npp.7.8.5.installer.x64.en-us.msi*, instead of Invoke-ApplicationInstall.ps1). If you do this and import the resulting intunewinapp file into the Intune portal, the install and uninstall command will have been automatically and correctly populated as though you were creating a standard Line of Business application.

You could leave the *uninstall* command in place. Then, delete the *install* command, and replace it with your new install command that invokes the PowerShell script.

As a bonus, when you then get to the "Detection Rules" tab and select "Manually Configure Detection Rules," selecting MSI as the rule type automatically configures the detection rule too.

Summary

In this chapter, you learned how to obtain the content prep tool and how to prepare your source files for conversion. You also learned how to complete the conversion. Finally, you learned that if you are deploying an MSI then you can automatically pre-populate the uninstall command line and detection in the Intune portal, by specifying the MSI name instead of the script name when preparing the content in the prep tool.

In the next chapter, you will learn about uninstalling an application.

CHAPTER 10

Uninstall an Application

You may need to uninstall an application as part of the existing deployment. In this chapter, you will delve a little deeper and learn how to remove an existing application before deploying a new one.

If you recall, in Chapter 2 you learned where in the registry you can find the uninstall GUIDS or commands. It can be cumbersome to find the information by manually browsing the registry, and PowerShell can help make this task a little easier.

PowerShell to the Rescue

Listing 10-1 shows a single line of PowerShell that can obtain the application GUIDs for all installed MSIs and Figure 10-1 shows the resulting output of the code execution. The correct GUID can then be used to uninstall the application using MSIEXEC as you learned from the earlier chapter.

Listing 10-1. Obtaining a list of all installed MSI GUIDs

```
Get-wmiobject Win32_Product | Format-Table
IdentifyingNumber, Name
```

Figure 10-1 shows sample output when running the command shown in Listing 10-1.

```
Windows PowerShell
PS C:\> get-wmiobject Win32_Product | Format-Table IdentifyingNumber, Name

IdentifyingNumber                        Name
-----------------                        ----
{F086BA42-A053-4A18-AC7E-9EECE26E1359}  TAL-Chorus-LX (VST3 64bit)
{49BAD20F-F5E9-4431-BCF0-F6068E5E19E0}  Repeater (64bit)
{90160000-008C-0000-1000-0000000FF1CE}  Office 16 Click-to-Run Extensibility Component
{90160000-007E-0000-1000-0000000FF1CE}  Office 16 Click-to-Run Licensing Component
{BD8C6100-7C7D-48DD-93BA-69F6828213FE}  Microsoft Visual C++ 2019 X86 Additional Runtime - 14.28.29914
{2D64E1A0-02C7-4AED-BCC6-3A5E5C91D6E2}  Steinberg HALion Sonic SE Standalone
{A5AB0D21-21BD-4D88-F097-02E8FC8C486A}  Steinberg Groove Agent SE 5
{2F802731-3731-453E-B30B-43B1BEED22AC}  teVirtualMIDI64
```

Figure 10-1.

The drawback to this method is that it can take a long time to populate the list (be patient) and it only retrieves MSI-installed applications.

Another method, again using PowerShell, searches both the 32-bit and 64-bit registry locations for all installed software, both MSI and Setup.exe, and will display the uninstall string if present. Listing 10-2 shows the code required to do this.

Listing 10-2. Searching the registry for uninstall information for both MSI and Setup.exe

```
$paths=@('HKLM:\SOFTWARE\WOW6432Node\Microsoft\Windows\↵
CurrentVersion\Uninstall\', 'HKLM:\SOFTWARE\Microsoft\↵
Windows\CurrentVersion\Uninstall\')
foreach($path in $paths){
    Get-ChildItem -Path $path | Get-ItemProperty | ↵
Select DisplayName, Publisher, InstallDate, ↵
DisplayVersion, UninstallString
}
```

When running this PowerShell code and examining the results you will notice some oddities. The MSI uninstall GUIDS are sometimes shown using the /i parameter and this signifies an installation. You will need to change this to /x to signify an uninstallation in your PowerShell code. Other MSI uninstall GUIDS may display the correct parameter.

Additionally, a lot of the setup.exe uninstall command lines are missing the switch for silent removal. Experience has taught me that generally, you will need to add /S at the end of the command for this, but make sure you test it first to ensure it works as expected. If not, use the tactics previously discussed in Chapter 2 to discover the silent switch.

Figure 10-2 demonstrates all these points – after running the PowerShell shown in Listing 10-2, the output displays *Java 8* with the correct MSIEXEC uninstall command line, a *Microsoft Visual C++ 2012 Redistributable (x86)* *setup.exe* missing the silent switch and a *Microsoft Visual C++ 2019 x86 Minimum Runtime MSI* with the incorrect uninstall parameter.

```
DisplayName       : Microsoft Visual C++ 2015-2019 Redistributable (x86) - 14.28.29914
Publisher         : Microsoft Corporation
InstallDate       :
DisplayVersion    : 14.28.29914.0
UninstallString   : "C:\ProgramData\Package Cache\{1b5476d9-ab8e-4b0d-b004-059a1bd5568b}\VC_redist.x86.exe" /uninstall

DisplayName       : Java 8 Update 341
Publisher         : Oracle Corporation
InstallDate       : 20220820
DisplayVersion    : 8.0.3410.10
UninstallString   : MsiExec.exe /X{26A24AE4-039D-4CA4-87B4-2F32180341F0}

DisplayName       : Microsoft Visual C++ 2012 Redistributable (x86) - 11.0.61030
Publisher         : Microsoft Corporation
InstallDate       :
DisplayVersion    : 11.0.61030.0
UninstallString   : "C:\ProgramData\Package Cache\{33d1fd90-4274-48a1-9bc1-97e33d9c2d6f}\vcredist_x86.exe" /uninstall

DisplayName       : Microsoft Visual C++ 2019 X86 Minimum Runtime - 14.28.29914
Publisher         : Microsoft Corporation
InstallDate       : 20211018
DisplayVersion    : 14.28.29914
UninstallString   : MsiExec.exe /I{42365A3A-622A-4EED-A727-FE192A794AFD}
```

Figure 10-2. *Example uninstall command lines. You may still need to make slight modifications to ensure they work*

In Practice

In an ideal world, before installing a new application, you should first discover if there is a previous version of the same application already installed. You can do this using a slightly modified detection rule. Then, if the previous version is detected, you would add the command to uninstall it.

All this would happen before the new application is installed and if you are using the example template that you learned how to use in Chapter 8, then this code would go in the *Invoke-PreInstallation* function.

Detecting the Old Application

Let us say that you must deploy Notepad++, version 8.4.4. You know that some systems may have an older Notepad++, version 8.4.3 installed, and this must be removed first. To do this you will use your existing application detection rule to detect the *old* version of the application and if found, uninstall it.

You must make one minor modification in your existing PowerShell detection rule for Notepad++. In a normal detection rule, you would use `Write-Host "Installed!"` to signify a successful detection of the installed application. Instead, you will substitute Write-Host with a modified install command you have already learned about in Chapter 6. Rather than installing an application though, you will uninstall it.

Example code on how to achieve this can be seen in Listing 10-3.

Listing 10-3. The detection and uninstallation code for removing an older version (version 8.43) of Notepad++. (Note the Write-Host cmdlet has been replaced by Start-Process)

```
$VersionNumber = '8.43'
$Executable = "notepad++.exe"
$Path = "${env:ProgramFiles}\notepad++"

If ((Get-item (Join-Path -Path $Path -ChildPath $Executable)↵
-ErrorAction SilentlyContinue).VersionInfo.ProductVersion ↵
-eq $VersionNumber) {
```

```
    Start-Process -FilePath "$env:ProgramFiles\notepad++
    \uninstall.exe" -ArgumentList ↩
"/S" -NoNewWindow -Wait
}
```

Adding to the Template

If you are using the example deployment template from Chapter 8, then you should place this code in the *Invoke-PreInstallation* function, and this is shown in Figure 10-3.

```
Invoke-ApplicationInstall.ps1* X
   1  ⊟Function Invoke-PreInstallation {
   2        $VersionNumber = '8.43'
   3        $Executable = "notepad++.exe"
   4        $Path = "${env:ProgramFiles}\notepad++"
   5
   6  ⊟      If ((Get-item (Join-Path -Path $Path -ChildPath $Execu
   7              start-process -FilePath "$env:ProgramFiles\notepad
   8        }
   9   }
  10
```

Figure 10-3. *Place your uninstall code in the Invoke-PreInstallation function*

Summary

In this chapter, you learned how to use PowerShell to easily obtain the application GUIDS or command lines that can be used to uninstall an application from a system.

You learned how to modify existing PowerShell detection rules to aid with the uninstallation process, and where to place the modified detection rule in the deployment template.

In the next chapter, you will see various examples of short code snippets that can be added to pre- or post-installation functions that will assist you in complex deployments.

CHAPTER 11

Pre- and Post-Code

Whether you use a template written by yourself, a quick deployment script, or are using the example deployment template demonstrated earlier in Chapter 8, you will, at some stage, need to perform some type of action before or after the application has been installed.

This chapter will demonstrate various code samples that will cover most of the fundamental pre- and post-deployment tasks you will come across.

If you are using the example deployment template provided by this book, then with little to no modification, each code sample can be placed directly into the pre- or post-functions (*Invoke-PreInstallation* and/or *Invoke-PostInstallation*).

Detect Office "Bitness"

This code snippet will detect if the installed version of Microsoft Office is 32-bit or 64-bit and I used it so much at one stage, that I embedded it into the deployment template itself, where it still remains.

It works by interrogating the registry for an installed version of Microsoft Office and, if found, attempts to read the "bitness" value and the associated data.

The data is listed in the registry as either *x86* or *x64* and will signify if the Microsoft Office installation is 32-bit (x86) or 64-bit (x64).

Listing 11-1 shows the full code required to achieve this detection.

© Owen Heaume 2022
O. Heaume, *Understanding Microsoft Intune*,
https://doi.org/10.1007/978-1-4842-8850-4_11

Listing 11-1. Detect Microsoft Office "bitness"

```
$OfficePaths = @('HKLM:\Software\Microsoft\Office','HKLM:\
Software\WOW6432Node\Microsoft\Office')
$OfficeVersions = @('14.0', '15.0', '16.0')

foreach ($Path in $OfficePaths) {
    foreach ($Version in $OfficeVersions) {
        try {
            Set-Location "$Path\$Version\Outlook" -ea
            stop -ev x
          $Bitness = Get-ItemPropertyValue -Name
          "Bitness" -ea stop -ev x
            switch ($bitness) {
             'x86' {$Is32Bit = $True}
                'x64' {$Is32Bit = $false}
            }
            break
        } catch {
            $Is32Bit = 'Unknown'
        }
    }
    if ($Is32Bit -eq $true -or $Is32Bit -eq $false) {break}
}
```

The code will set a variable named $Is32Bit to one of three values:

1. $True: Microsoft Office is a 32-bit installation.

2. $False: Microsoft Office is a 64-bit installation.

3. "Unknown": Microsoft Office may not be installed.

It is then up to you how you use the resulting information contained in the variable $Is32Bit.

Note   This detection relies on Microsoft Outlook being installed as part of the Office installation. If Outlook has not been installed, then this code will not work.

Detect Operating System Architecture

Detecting if the installed Windows operating system is 32-bit or 64-bit can be determined with a single line of PowerShell.

The operating system is queried and the return value (either "64-bit" or "32-bit") is returned and stored in the variable $OSArchitecture.

The code for this can be seen in Listing 11-2.

Listing 11-2. Detecting the operating system architecture

```
$OSArchitecture = (Get-CimInstance -ClassName ↵
CIM_OperatingSystem).OSArchitecture
```

Obtaining the Current Logged-in Username

Even though scripts may be deployed using the SYSTEM account, it is still possible to query who the currently logged-in user is and, once again, it is achieved using a single line of PowerShell.

Listing 11-3 shows the code for obtaining this information, which is then stored in the variable named $LoggedInUser.

Listing 11-3. Obtaining the currently logged-in username

```
$LoggedInUser = (Get-CimInstance -ClassName ↵
CIM_ComputerSystem).username | Split-Path -Leaf
```

Note   You may be wondering why the PowerShell environment variable, $env:UserName is not used. This is because if the script is being deployed in the system context, it would return the account being used that is running the script, and that is not the user! In most application deployment cases, the script will be running in the system context and therefore an alternative method of obtaining the logged-in username must be used.

Copying Files

Copying files is a common task as part of the pre- or post-application deployment and it is achieved using a single PowerShell cmdlet, Copy-Item.

How you use the cmdlet will depend on how the files have been initially structured (see the section "Adding the Content" in Chapter 9 for a refresher).

Unstructured Method

The unstructured method can be used when all files from the preparation phase have been placed all together in a single directory.

In this example scenario, let us assume several files require copying to the \Windows\Wallpaper directory onto the target computer and another file to the Windows\Ini directory.

Figure 11-1 shows what the file structure may look like in this scenario.

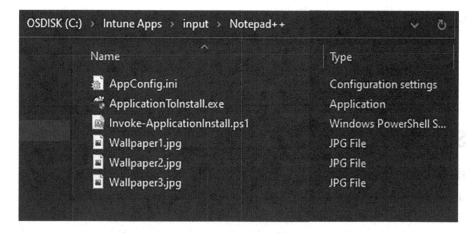

Figure 11-1. *All files are in the same root directory*

Copy-Item along with the -Include switch will allow you to achieve the desired outcome.

By using the -include switch it is possible to filter the copy operation to only those files you are interested in; in this case, files with the .jpg extension.

Even though a mixture of file types is in the root directory, only jpg files will be copied to the destination as shown by the code in Listing 11-4.

Listing 11-4. Copying only the jpg files

```
Copy-Item -Path "$PSScriptRoot\*.*" -Destination ↵
"$env:SystemRoot\Wallpaper" -Include '*.jpg' ↵
-ErrorAction SilentlyContinue
```

To copy only files with the .ini extension change the -Include filter as shown in Listing 11-5.

Listing 11-5. Copying only the INI file

```
Copy-Item -Path "$PSScriptRoot\*.*" -Destination ↵
"$env:SystemRoot\ini" -Include '*.ini' -ErrorAction ↵
SilentlyContinue
```

Structured Method

If you have prepared your deployment files using a structured approach, then you will not need to use the -include switch as all the different file types will be separated already.

An example of structured file placement is shown in Figure 11-2.

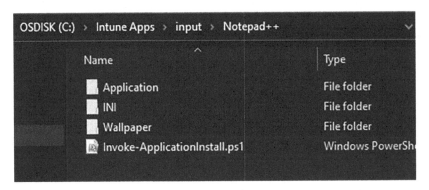

Figure 11-2. *Files of the same file type are contained in separate subdirectories*

To copy files in subdirectories you must reference the path in the -path parameter of the Copy-Item cmdlet.

Listing 11-6 demonstrates this.

Listing 11-6. Copying all the jpg files contained in the Wallpaper subdirectory to /Windows/Wallpaper on the target computer

```
Copy-Item -Path "$PSScriptRoot\Wallpaper\*.*" -Destination ↵
"$env:SystemRoot\Wallpaper" -ErrorAction SilentlyContinue
```

Continuing the example, the same procedure is used for the INI file by referencing their location in the -Path parameter. Listing 11-7 demonstrates this.

Listing 11-7. Copying only the INI files that are in a subdirectory

```
Copy-Item -Path "$PSScriptRoot\ini\*.*" -Destination ↩
"$env:SystemRoot\ini" -ErrorAction SilentlyContinue
```

Register/Unregister DLL Files

To register or unregister a DLL (Dynamic Link Library) file you must use the built-in executable, *Regsvr32.exe* found at \Windows\system32 as shown in Figure 11-3.

Figure 11-3 shows the location of the executable.

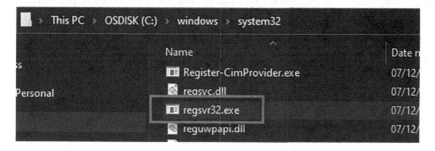

Figure 11-3.

You can read all about Regsvr32.exe on the Microsoft documentation found at the following URL: *https://docs.microsoft.com/en-us/ windows-server/administration/windows-commands/regsvr32*

Register a DLL

The following example shows how to register a DLL that is in the root application directory (unstructured file placement).

Edit the variable $DllFileName to reflect the name of the DLL file you wish to register. Listing 11-8 shows an example of registering a DLL named *MyDLL.dll*.

Listing 11-8. Registering a DLL file

```
$DLLFileName = "MyDLL.dll"
Start-Process -FilePath ↵
"$env:SystemRoot\System32\regsvr32.exe" -ArgumentList "/S ↵
""$PSScriptRoot\$DLLFileName""" -Wait -NoNewWindow
```

If you have used a structured file placement method as part of your previous application preparation, change the -ArgumentList parameter to reflect the source path.

For example, if the DLL files are in a subdirectory of the root named *DLL*, then the code will look as shown in Listing 11-9.

Listing 11-9. Registering a DLL contained in a subdirectory

```
$DLLFileName = "MyDLL.dll" ↵
Start-Process -FilePath
"$env:SystemRoot\System32\regsvr32.exe" -ArgumentList "/S ↵
""$PSScriptRoot\DLL\$DLLFileName""" -Wait -NoNewWindow
```

Unregister a DLL

To unregister a DLL, you must add the /U parameter as per the Microsoft documentation referenced earlier. Listing 11-10 shows this additional switch in use.

Listing 11-10. Unregistering a DLL using the /U switch

```
$DLLFileName = "MyDLL.dll" ↩
Start-Process -FilePath ↩
"$env:SystemRoot\System32\regsvr32.exe" -ArgumentList "/S /U ↩
""$WorkingDir\$DLLFileName""" -Wait -NoNewWindow
```

Summary

In this chapter, you were shown various code snippets that can be useful in the pre-deployment or post-deployment phase of a scripted application install.

In the next and final chapter, an example deployment scenario will be given for you to follow from start to finish, reinforcing some of the key concepts this book has covered.

CHAPTER 12

Example Scenario

In this chapter, you will learn the step-by-step process for completing an advanced application deployment using some of the techniques demonstrated in this book and using the example deployment template presented in Chapter 8.

Notepad++

You have been approached by your manager with the following application task:

1. Make available version 8.4.3.0 of Notepad++ to all users.

2. Before installing, uninstall version 8.4.2.0 of Notepad++ if already installed.

3. Place a copy of the custom-written Notepad++ manual in the logged-in user's documents folder as part of the installation.

Obtain the Installer

The first step is to download the application install file and determine what type it is: an EXE installer or MSI.

© Owen Heaume 2022
O. Heaume, *Understanding Microsoft Intune*,
https://doi.org/10.1007/978-1-4842-8850-4_12

Visiting the Notepad++ website and downloading the 64-bit version resulted in a single setup.exe file. There were no available MSI installers to download. (See Figure 12-1)

Figure 12-1. *The downloaded 64-bit Notepad++ setup executable*

MSI Extraction

Knowing that deploying an MSI file can be easier and offer more flexibility, an attempt to extract an MSI is made by right-clicking the EXE application and extracting the contents to a directory using 7-Zip. This is shown in Figure 12-2.

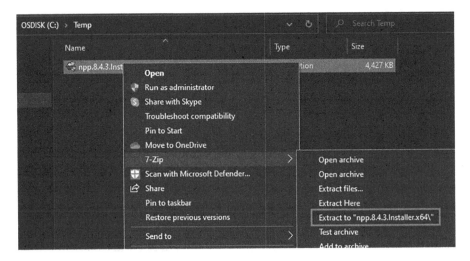

Figure 12-2. *Attempting to extract an MSI from the EXE installer using 7-Zip*

Looking at the resulting extraction, unfortunately, this time, revealed no MSI that could be used. This would have to be a setup.exe deployment. Well, you cannot win them all. Figure 12-3 shows the results of the extraction.

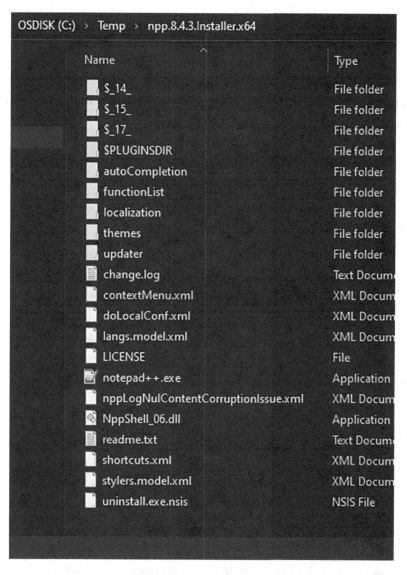

Figure 12-3. *The results of extracting the contents of the EXE. No luck this time!*

Determine the Install and Uninstall Commands

Deploying and uninstalling Notepad++ must be achieved using a silent install.

Find the Silent Install Parameter

Experience has proven, in the case of EXE installation files, that using the /S parameter to initiate a silent installation works in the majority, but not all, cases.

It is quick to try: in an administrative command prompt, the EXE installer is run with the added /S parameter.

Changing to the same directory containing the EXE installer, the following command was typed in the command console:
npp.8.4.3.Installer.x64.exe /S

Figure 12-4 demonstrates this.

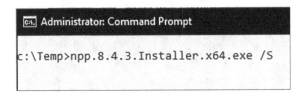

Figure 12-4. *Testing a well-known silent install parameter*

Note   All testing should be completed on a test computer. I like to test on a VM (Virtual Machine) as I can "reset" it after every test.

Well, what do you know? In a couple of seconds, Notepad++ had installed silently. Using the well-known switch was a success on this occasion.

If this had failed, the parameter /? could have been tried and failing that, an Internet search.

The test installation was then uninstalled via Control Panel.

Note   I tried using the /? to see if there was any built-in help –
alas there was not. I then performed an Internet search and
multiple results mentioned the silent install parameter required for
Notepad++.

Find the Silent Uninstall Parameter

One of the requirements is to uninstall the previously installed version of
Notepad++ before installation of the new one.

The previous version of Notepad++ (version 8.4.2) was installed
manually to the test computer, and PowerShell code to interrogate the
registry for the uninstall command was executed.

This is the same code shown in Listing 10-2 (Chapter 10). For
convenience, it is repeated here in Listing 12-1.

Listing 12-1. Searching the registry for uninstall information for
both MSI and Setup.exe

```
$paths=@('HKLM:\SOFTWARE\WOW6432Node\Microsoft\Windows\↩
CurrentVersion\Uninstall\', 'HKLM:\SOFTWARE\Microsoft\ ↩
Windows\CurrentVersion\Uninstall\')
foreach($path in $paths){
    Get-ChildItem -Path $path | Get-ItemProperty | ↩
Select DisplayName, Publisher, InstallDate, ↩
DisplayVersion, UninstallString
}
```

The results of the code execution displayed the uninstall command for Notepad++ (version 8.4.2) as shown in Figure 12-5.

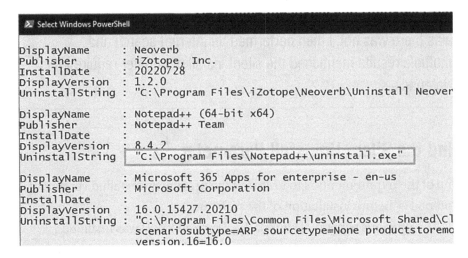

Figure 12-5. *The uninstall command for Notepad++*

If you recall from Chapter 10, many uninstall commands miss the silent switch required for our purposes. As we have already successfully discovered the silent *install* parameter, it is more than likely that the same parameter can be used for silent *uninstall*. It is time for another test.

Once again in an administrative command prompt on the test computer, the newly discovered uninstall string was then typed in: "c:\ program files\notepad++\uninstall.exe" /S as shown in Figure 12-6.

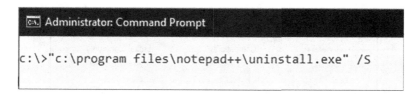

Figure 12-6. *Testing the uninstall command line*

The test was completed successfully and Notepad++ was silently uninstalled.

Now that both the silent install and uninstall command lines had been discovered, it was time to create the detection rule for the application installation.

The Application Detection Rule

To detect the new installation of Notepad++, a PowerShell detection rule based on the version number of the installed executable will be used.

Although this type of rule doesn't require PowerShell as it can be done natively within Intune, it will be required when it comes to creating the PowerShell code for uninstalling the previous version of Notepad++ later, so we may as well create it now and use it as the primary application detection method too.

Checking the Details tab on the property page of the Notepad++ executable shows that the product version is 8.43. (See Figure 12-7)

Figure 12-7. *The product version of the installed executable is 8.43*

The code from Listing 4-6 (Chapter 4) will be used as the detection rule, as this will detect the product version on an installed executable.

The three variables $versionNumber, $executable, and $path have been updated with the Notepad++ details, and the final code is presented in Listing 12-2.

Listing 12-2. The completed detection rule for Notepad++ version 8.4.3

```
$versionNumber = '8.43'
$executable = "notepad++.exe"
$path = "$env:ProgramFiles\notepad++"

If ((Get-item (Join-Path -Path $path -ChildPath ↵
$executable) -ErrorAction SilentlyContinue).VersionInfo.↵
ProductVersion -eq $VersionNumber) {↵
    Write-Host "Detected!"
}
```

A quick sanity check was undertaken to ensure the executable was correctly detected by running the script on a test computer that had Notepad++ version 8.43 installed, as shown in Figure 12-8.

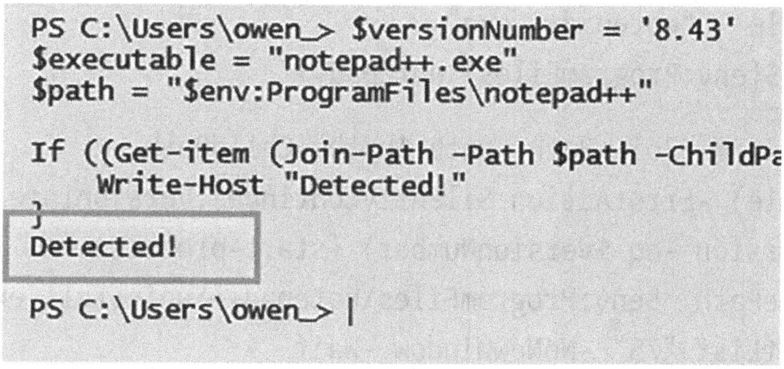

```
PS C:\Users\owen_> $versionNumber = '8.43'
$executable = "notepad++.exe"
$path = "$env:ProgramFiles\notepad++"

If ((Get-item (Join-Path -Path $path -ChildPa
    Write-Host "Detected!"
}
Detected!

PS C:\Users\owen_> |
```

Figure 12-8. *Testing the detection rule*

The final detection rule was saved as *Notepad++_Detection.ps1* ready for use later.

The Uninstall Code

With the detection script already tested and written, and the uninstall command line to hand, creating the code for uninstalling the previous version of Notepad++ (version 8.42) is next.

As you learned in Chapter 10, this would be a simple case of modifying an existing detection rule so that instead of using Write-Host to signify a successful installation, the Start-Process cmdlet would be used instead to instigate the uninstall command line obtained earlier.

Listing 12-3 presents the final code for detecting the previous version of Notepad++ and if detected, uninstall it.

Listing 12-3. The final code for detecting and removing Notepad++ version 8.42

```
$versionNumber = '8.42'
$executable = "notepad++.exe"
$path = "${env:ProgramFiles}\notepad++"

If ((Get-item (Join-Path -Path $path -ChildPath ↩
$executable) -ErrorAction SilentlyContinue).VersionInfo.↩
ProductVersion -eq $versionNumber) {start-process ↩
    -FilePath "$env:ProgramFiles\notepad++\uninstall.exe" ↩
 -ArgumentList "/S" -NoNewWindow -Wait
}
```

To verify the code worked as intended, it was manually executed on a computer with the older version of Notepad++ installed (version 8.42). The code detected the installed application correctly and silently removed it.

Source File Placement

All source files will be placed in relevant subfolders using the structured approach seen in Chapter 5.

The Notepad++ executable will be placed in an "Application" subdirectory and the Manual.pdf will be placed in a "PDF" subfolder. The deployment template PowerShell script will be in the root. The results of this structured placement are shown in Figure 12-9.

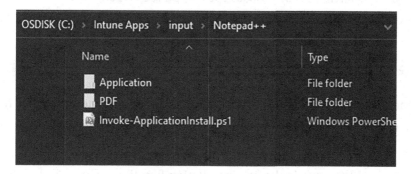

Figure 12-9. *A structured file placement for the source files has been used*

The File Copy Code

Part of the deployment criteria set by the manager is to include a copy of the custom-written Notepad++ manual in the currently logged-in user's documents folder.

Now that it has been determined that all source files are placed using a structured approach, it is a simple task of modifying the existing code shown in Listing 11-6 (Chapter 11).

The code will also need to obtain the currently logged-in user (using the same code as seen in Listing 11-3 (Chapter 11)), and this will be used to create the path to the file copy destination directory.

Listing 12-4 presents the final code that will be used for copying Manual.pdf into the logged-in user's documents directory.

Listing 12-4. The final code will copy Manual.pdf into the logged-in user's documents folder

```
$loggedInUser = (Get-CimInstance -ClassName ↵
CIM_ComputerSystem).username | Split-Path -Leaf
Copy-Item -Path ".\PDF\Manual.pdf" -Destination ↵
"C:\Users\$loggedInUser\Documents"
```

The Deployment Template

All the information required to populate the deployment template has now been obtained. The following actions will be performed:

1. The code for uninstalling the previous Notepad++ will execute in the pre-installation function. (See Figure 12-10)

```
 1 ⊟Function Invoke-PreInstallation {
 2        $VersionNumber = '8.42'
 3        $Executable = "notepad++.exe"
 4        $Path = "${env:ProgramFiles}\notepad++"
 5
 6 ⊟      If ((Get-item (Join-Path -Path $Path -ChildPath $Executable) -ErrorActic
 7            start-process -FilePath "$env:ProgramFiles\notepad++\uninstall.exe"
 8        }
 9  └}
10
```

Figure 12-10. *Detecting if Notepad++ version 8.4.2.0 has been installed and if so, remove it. The code has been placed into the Pre-Installation function of the template*

2. All computers in the company are 64-bit operating systems, and so the install code will be placed in the relevant location in the deployment template. (See Figure 12-11)

```
89
90  switch ($obj.OSIs64Bit) {
91      $True {start-process -FilePath ".\Application\npp.8.4.3.Installer.x64.exe"
92      default {start-process -FilePath "$ENV:SystemRoot\System32\msiexec.exe" -Ar
93  }
94  }
```

Figure 12-11. *Adding the code to install the new Notepad++*
application

3. The code to copy the Manual.pdf will execute after
the application has been installed and therefore will
be placed in the post-installation function.
(See Figure 12-12)

```
10
11  function Invoke-PostInstallation {
12      # Anything you do here will occur **after** the installation...
13      # Perhaps copy some files, register some DLL's or anything else
14      $LoggedInUser = (Get-CimInstance -ClassName CIM_ComputerSystem).
15      copy-item -Path ".\PDF\Manual.pdf" -Destination "C:\Users\$Logge
16  }
17
```

Figure 12-12. *The Post-Installation function contains the code for*
copying Manual.pdf to the logged-in user's documents folder

Application Uninstallation

The application uninstall code is copied to the *Invoke-PreInstallation*
function in the deployment template.

Notepad++ Installation

By default, when this template is executed, it will install an application
based on the detected installed operating system being 64-bit.

The code to install Notepad++ is copied to the $OSIs64Bit = $True
section of the deployment template.

The full installation command line used is presented in Listing 12-5.

Listing 12-5. The installation command line used to install Notepad++

```
Start-Process -FilePath ".\Application\npp.8.4.3.Installer. ↵
x64.exe" -ArgumentList "/S" -NoNewWindow -Wait
```

Post-Installation

The code to copy Manual.pdf to the currently logged-in user's documents folder is copied to the *Invoke-PostInstallation* function in the deployment template.

The full code used for the post-installation is presented in Listing 12-6.

Listing 12-6. The full code used to perform the file copy operation. Note the use of an environment variable piped to Split-Path to obtain the root drive letter

```
$loggedInUser = (Get-CimInstance -ClassName ↵
CIM_ComputerSystem).username | Split-Path -Leaf
Copy-Item -Path ".\PDF\Manual.pdf" -Destination ↵
"$($env:windir | Split-Path ↵
-Parent)\Users\$loggedInUser\Documents"
```

Dry Run

A dry run of the script is performed next to ensure that everything functions as expected.

For the test, a computer is installed with Notepad++ version 8.42. and when the script is run, it should remove it and replace it with Notepad version 8.43. Additionally, Manual.pdf should be found in the documents folder.

To run the test, the entire script is loaded into the PowerShell ISE on the test computer, and the location is manually changed to the application root directory that contains the source files (for example by typing:

`Set-Location "C:\Intune Apps\input\Notepad++"` in the console window of the ISE), and then executed by pressing F5 to run the script.

If everything went as expected, it is time to package up the source files into an intunewin file ready for uploading into Intune.

Create the Intunewin File

Ensuring that your completed deployment template (Invoke-ApplicationInstall.ps1) has been copied to the root application folder of all the source files, (as shown in Figure 12-13), it is now time to create the intunewin file.

***Figure 12-13.** The source files are ready for the conversion process*

Begin by launching the IntuneWinAppUtil.exe and filling in the required prerequisite information, as seen earlier in Chapter 9. Figure 12-14 shows the information entered for this Notepad++ scenario.

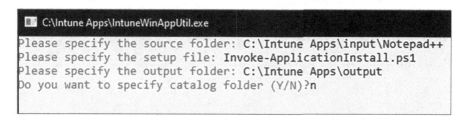

***Figure 12-14.** All the prerequisite information has been entered ready to create the intunewin file*

After a few moments, the intunewin file has been created as shown in Figure 12-15.

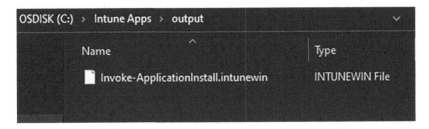

Figure 12-15. *The resulting intunewin file*

Application Deployment

It is now time to create the application in Intune, so log in to *https://endpoint.microsoft.com* and create a new Win32 app. (See Figure 12-16)

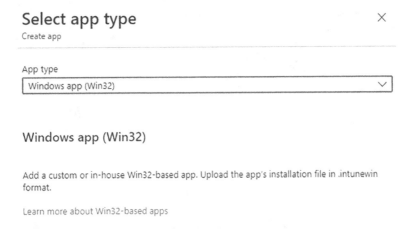

Figure 12-16. *Creating a new Win32 app in the Intune portal*

Next, click "Select app package file." (See Figure 12-17)

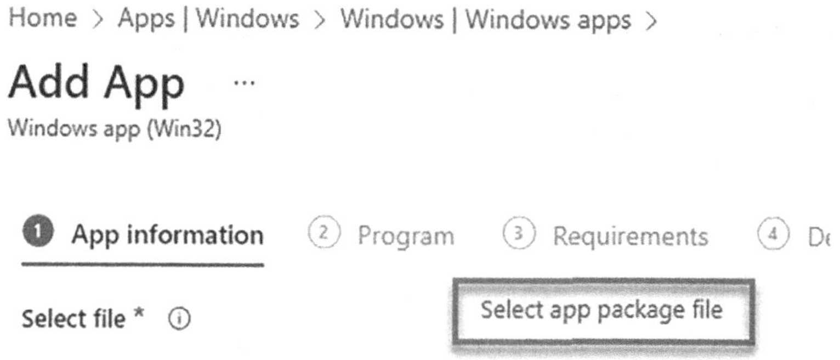

Home > Apps | Windows > Windows | Windows apps >

Add App   ⋯

Windows app (Win32)

1 App information   ② Program   ③ Requirements   ④ Dₑ

Select file * ⓘ   Select app package file

Figure 12-17. *Click the "Select app package file" link*

Click the blue folder icon and browse to the Invoke-Application.
intunewin file created earlier. (See Figure 12-18)

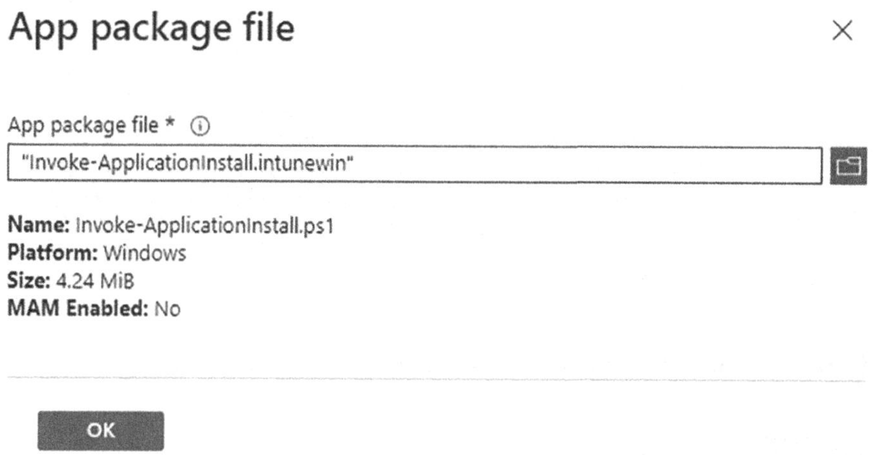

App package file   ✕

App package file * ⓘ

"Invoke-ApplicationInstall.intunewin"   🗁

Name: Invoke-ApplicationInstall.ps1
Platform: Windows
Size: 4.24 MiB
MAM Enabled: No

OK

Figure 12-18. *The intunewin file has been selected*

App Information

Complete the app information page as shown in Figure 12-19.

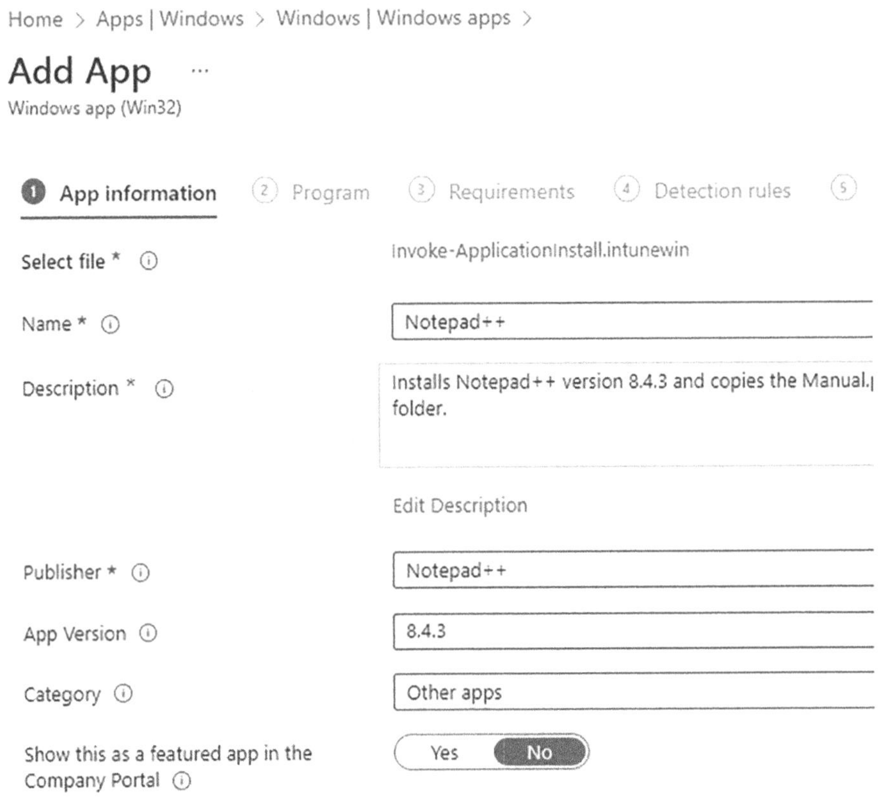

Home > Apps | Windows > Windows | Windows apps >

Add App   ⋯
Windows app (Win32)

| ① App information | ② Program | ③ Requirements | ④ Detection rules | ⑤ |

Select file *   ⓘ

Invoke-ApplicationInstall.intunewin

Name *   ⓘ

Notepad++

Description *   ⓘ

Installs Notepad++ version 8.4.3 and copies the Manual.
folder.

Edit Description

Publisher *   ⓘ

Notepad++

App Version   ⓘ

8.4.3

Category   ⓘ

Other apps

Show this as a featured app in the
Company Portal   ⓘ

Yes   No

Figure 12-19. *Fill in the required App information fields*

Program

The deployment template is executed using an entry point, and therefore
uses the command line for installing a script with an entry point you
learned about in Chapter 7.

Complete the *Install command* and *Uninstall command* text field with the same command line:

```
"C:\Windows\Sysnative\WindowsPowerShell\v1.0\PowerShell.exe" ↵
-noprofile -executionpolicy bypass -file ↵
.\Invoke-ApplicationInstall.ps1
```

This is shown in Figure 12-20.

Home > Apps | Windows > Windows | Windows apps >

Add App   ···
Windows app (Win32)

✓ App information	② Program	③ Requirements	④ Detection rules	⑤ Dependencies	⑥ Supersed

Specify the commands to install and uninstall this app:

Install command * ⓘ	"C:\Windows\Sysnative\WindowsPowerShell\v1.0\PowerShell.exe" -noprofile -e... ✓
Uninstall command * ⓘ	"C:\Windows\Sysnative\WindowsPowerShell\v1.0\PowerShell.exe" -noprofile -e... ✓
Install behavior ⓘ	[System] User
Device restart behavior ⓘ	App install may force a device restart ⌄

Specify return codes to indicate post-installation behavior:

Figure 12-20. *Complete the install and uninstall commands and ensure "Install behavior" is set to "system" so that the script runs in the system, not the user, context*

Requirements

Next, add the application requirements that meet your organizational needs. (See Figure 12-21)

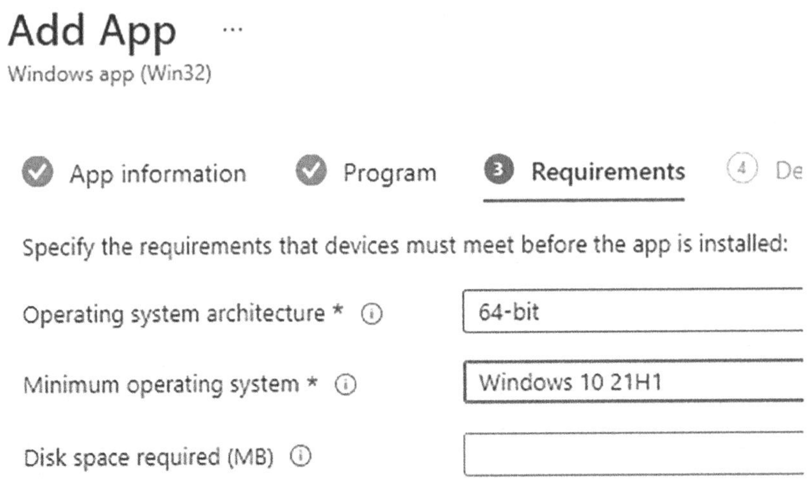

Add App   ⋯
Windows app (Win32)

✓ App information   ✓ Program   ❸ Requirements   ④ De

Specify the requirements that devices must meet before the app is installed:

Operating system architecture * ⓘ | 64-bit |

Minimum operating system * ⓘ | Windows 10 21H1 |

Disk space required (MB) ⓘ | |

Figure 12-21. Adding the application requirements

Detection Rules

Click the drop-down selector next to "Rules format" and choose "Use a custom detection script." Then click the blue folder icon and browse to the detection script saved earlier. (See Figure 12-22)

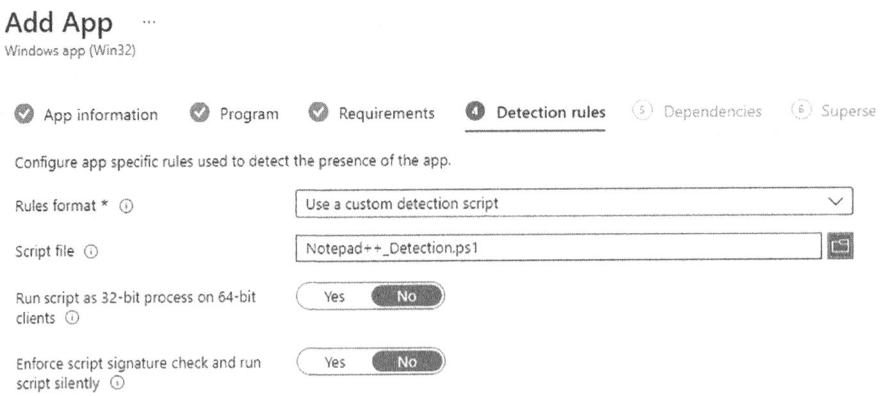

Add App   ⋯
Windows app (Win32)

✓ App information   ✓ Program   ✓ Requirements   ❹ Detection rules   ⑤ Dependencies   ⑥ Superse

Configure app specific rules used to detect the presence of the app.

Rules format * ⓘ | Use a custom detection script   ∨ |

Script file ⓘ | Notepad++_Detection.ps1   🗀 |

Run script as 32-bit process on 64-bit clients ⓘ   (Yes **No**)

Enforce script signature check and run script silently ⓘ   (Yes **No**)

Figure 12-22. Selecting a custom PowerShell detection script

Dependencies

This application does not have any dependencies so click next to continue. (See Figure 12-23)

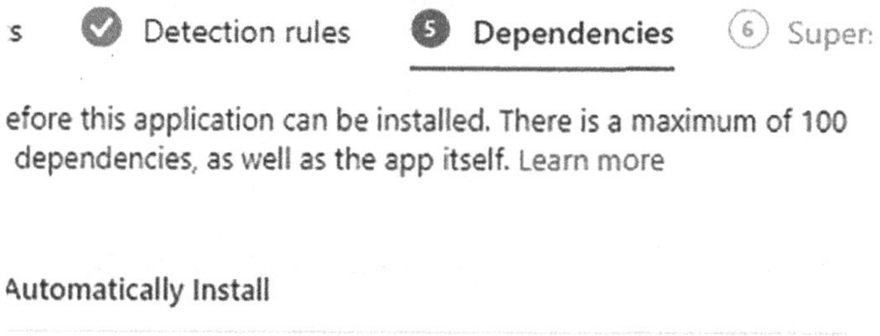

s   ✓ Detection rules   **⑤ Dependencies**   ⑥ Super:

efore this application can be installed. There is a maximum of 100 dependencies, as well as the app itself. Learn more

Automatically Install

Figure 12-23. *There are no dependencies to add so click next to continue*

Supersedence

This application does not use supersedence so click next to continue. (See Figure 12-24)

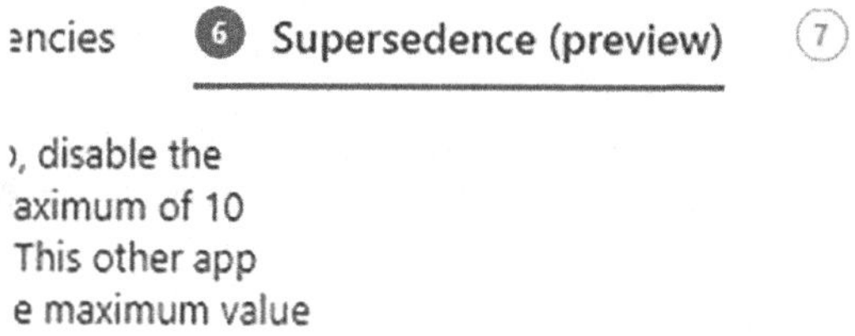

ɛncies   **⑥ Supersedence (preview)**   ⑦

), disable the
aximum of 10
This other app
e maximum value

Figure 12-24. *There are no supersedence rules to add for this application, so click next to continue*

Assignments

This application will be made *available* to users.

It's always best to assign the application to a test group first to make sure it works as expected. On the assignments page, under "Available for enrolled devices" browse to and select your test group. (See Figure 12-25)

+ Add group ⓘ + Add all users ⓘ + Add all devices ⓘ

Available for enrolled devices ⓘ

Group mode	Group
⊕ Included	az_col_testOH_usr

+ Add group ⓘ + Add all users ⓘ

Figure 12-25. *Make the application available to a test group first*

Note If you make an application "available," then you must assign it to a group containing user objects, not computers.

Review and Create

On the final "Review and create" page, you can see the summary showing the application install and uninstall commands as shown in Figure 12-26.

Program

Install command	"C:\Windows\Sysnative\WindowsPowerShell\v1.0\PowerShell.exe" -noprofile -executionpolicy bypass -file .\Invoke-ApplicationInstall.ps1
Uninstall command	"C:\Windows\Sysnative\WindowsPowerShell\v1.0\PowerShell.exe" -noprofile -executionpolicy bypass -file .\Invoke-ApplicationInstall.ps1
Install behavior	System
Device restart behavior	App install may force a device restart
Return codes	0 Success
	1707 Success

Figure 12-26. *A summary of all the options chosen during application creation. Here you can see the install and uninstall command lines in their entirety*

You have now created and deployed the Notepad++ application, meeting all the criteria set by the manager.

Once you have confirmed it deploys and installs correctly to the users in your test group, you can make it widely available by deploying it to all users.

Log File

The application deployment template contains a basic log writing feature.

The log file is named, *Invoke-ApplicationInstall* and can be found on each computer that has installed the application. It is located in .\ *Windows\temp*. (See Figure 12-27)

OSDISK (C:) > Windows > temp
Name
Type
Invoke-ApplicationInstall.log
Text Docume
MpCmdRun.log
Text Docume
MpCopyAccelerator.log
Text Docume

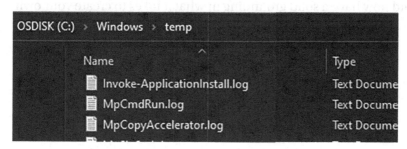

***Figure 12-27.** The location of the log file: Invoke-ApplicationInstall.log*

The contents of the log are shown in Figure 12-28.

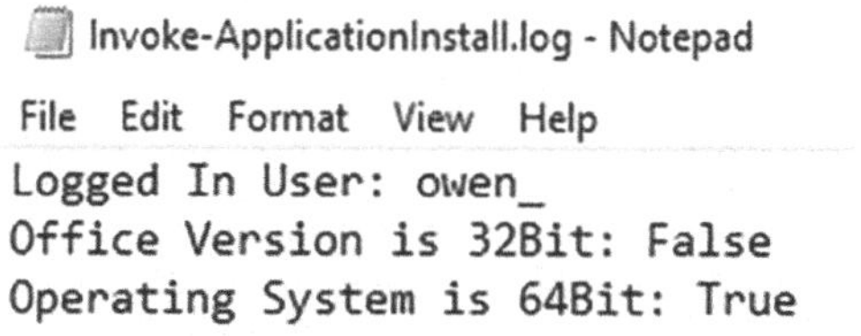

Invoke-ApplicationInstall.log - Notepad
File Edit Format View Help
Logged In User: owen_
Office Version is 32Bit: False
Operating System is 64Bit: True

***Figure 12-28.** The contents of the log file. This can easily be enhanced to include almost anything you are able to think of!*

Summary

In this final chapter, you learned how to install an application using a PowerShell deployment template, from start to finish.

Not only did the final application template deploy Notepad++, but it also detected and removed the previous version if it was present, and copied a PDF to the logged-in user's documents folder, using the pre- and post-functions. Finally, you learned how to complete the essential fields in the Win32 app creation wizard in the Intune portal.

It discussed many techniques covered in earlier chapters, and you should now have a solid grounding in what it takes to create your own deployment scripts or template.

Index

A

Application detection method, 161
Automatic variable, 80, 81, 85, 95

B

Branching detection rules, 72

C

Cmdlets, 5
    Copy-Item, 14
    get-command, 5
    Get-Item, 14
    Get-Location, 10
    Get-Process, 7, 10
    New-Item, 13
    New-ItemProperty, 13
    parameters, 8
    pipeline, 8
    Set-Location, 10
    Start-Process, 12
    Stop-Process, 11, 12
    Test-Path, 15
    Write-Host, 9
Copying files
    structured method, 150, 151
    unstructured method, 148–150
Copy-Item, 14, 82, 83, 148–150
Custom detection
    file, 66, 67
    registry, 69, 70
    WindowsSystem32, 65

D

Deployment script, 87
    entry point, 103
        install command, 104
        with parameters, 104
        without parameters, 103
    function, 105
        accepts parameters, 107
        deploying script, two
           functions, 108
        install command, 106, 108
        without parameters, 106
    install command, 102
    top to bottom, 102
Deployment template
    applicationinstall
        begin block, 123, 124
        end block, 126
        process block, 125, 126

© Owen Heaume 2022
O. Heaume, *Understanding Microsoft Intune*,
https://doi.org/10.1007/978-1-4842-8850-4

Deployment template (*cont.*)

    command line, 127, 128

    postinstallation, 123

    preinstallation, 122

    switch, 127

Detect

    currently logged-in
        username, 147

    Microsoft Office, bitness, 146

    Windows operating system, 147

Detection rules, 163

    creation process, 50, 51

    data pair, 62–64

    executable presence, 56

    executable version, 56, 57

        build number, 58, 60

        file, 59

        product, 59

    file/folder presence, 55

    Microsoft
        interpreting table, 49

    PowerShell, 47

    registry subkey, 61, 62

    registry value, 62–64

    script works, 53, 54

    SilentlyContinue, 51, 52

    Write-Host, 50

Detection script works, 53, 54

Dry run, 168–169

Dynamic Link Library (DLL)

    register, 151, 152

    unregister, 152

E

End User License Agreement
    (EULA), 29

Environment variables, 25–27,
    56, 94, 168

Executable detection, 56

F

File location, 79

    automatic variable, 81

    PowerShell syntax, 80

    PowerShell version 3, 81

-filepath parameter, 94

Flat-file placement, 81–82

G, H

Get-Location, 9–10, 15

Get-Process, 7, 8, 10–11, 99

I

Intunewin format, 129

    adding content, 133

    content prep
        tool, 129–131

    prepare to Prep, 131, 132

    source files, 134–136

    ZIP file, 131

Invoke-PreInstallation function,
    142, 143, 167

J, K

Java runtime executables (JRE), 42

L

Log file, 29–31, 126, 177

M

Mimecast, 73–75, 96
MSI
  installer, 97
  properties, 97
  setup, 98
Msiexec
  GUID
    64-bit installations, 35, 36
    32-bit installations, 34, 35
  help file, 23
  location, 24
  parameters, 21
    installation, 27
    no restart, 28
    silent install, 28
    uninstall, 28
  properties
    ERPSYSTEM, 30
    logfile, 29
    values, 31–33
  uses, 21
  $ENV, 25, 26
MSI-installed applications, 140

N, O

New-Item, 13
Notepad++ website
  app information, 172
  application deployment, 170
  application detection
    method, 161–163
  application uninstall code, 167
  app package, 171
  assignments, 175, 176
  copy file, 165, 166
  dependencies, 175
  deployment
    template, 166, 167
  detection rules, 174
  dry run, 168
  final code, 164
  install/uninstall, 158, 164, 167
  intunewin file, 169, 170
  log file, 177
  MSI extraction, 156, 157
  obtain, 156
  post-installation, 167, 168
  program, 172, 173
  requirements, 173
  review and create, 176, 177
  silent install
    parameter, 158, 159
  silent uninstall
    parameter, 159–161
  source files, 165
  supersedence, 175

P, Q

Pop-Location, 89, 90, 92

PowerShell code, 140

    detect old application, 142

    uninstall command lines, 141

    uninstall information, 140

PowerShell deployment script, 28, 81,

    84, 85, 101, 132, 134, 135, 137

PowerShell script, 23, 25, 81, 99,

    100, 115, 165

    64-bit version, 101

    32-bit version, 100, 101

PowerShell template, 2, 118

    ISE, 2, 4

Pre/post-functions, 145

$PSScriptRoot, 81, 84–87, 95

Push-Location, 89–92, 124

R

Reference files

    beginning of script, 84

    flat structure, 85

    subdirectories, 85, 86

Registry subkey, 61–62, 65, 124

Remote Server Administration

    Tools (RSAT), 109–115

S

Sage Enterprise

    Management, 31–33

Scripting

    finally block, 18

    if/else statement, 19

    ISE, 16

    try/catch block, 18

Set-Location, 9–10, 15, 84–87,

    89, 94, 124

setup.exe file

    help, 40

    install/uninstall

        parameters, 39, 40

    internet search, 41

    MSI

        detective skills, 45

        location, 45

        manual install, 42

        manual running, 43

        Temp directory, 44

        7-zip, 42

SilentlyContinue, 51–53, 64

Spaces, 85, 96–97

Start-Process, 12–13, 93, 94, 97, 164

Start-Process cmdlet

    -argumentlist

        minimum information, 95

    -nonewwindow, 96

    parameters

        EXE, 94

        -filepath, 94

        MSIEXEC, 94

    -wait, 96

Stop-Process, 8, 11–12

Structured file placement, 82, 83

Structured method, 150–151

Supersedence, 175

Sysnative, 100, 101

T

Test-Path, 15, 19, 20

U, V

Unstructured method, 148–150

W, X, Y, Z

Write-Host, 9, 49, 50, 54, 55, 88, 91, 92, 142

Printed in the United States
by Baker & Taylor Publisher Services